Project AIR FORCE
Arroyo Center
National Defense Research

NOT WITH A BANG BUT A WHIMPER

Western Europe Approaches the Third Millenium

ROBERT A. LEVINE

Prepared for the
United States Air Force
United States Army
Office of the Secretary of Defense

RAND

This report on the state of Western Europe as it approaches the year 2000 utilizes information from a number of sources: a meeting of the West/West Agenda in Berlin; direct observations of economic activity and social change in eastern Germany; conversations with government officials and others in Paris; a conference in Brussels on Foreign Direct Investment, sponsored by RAND's European-American Center; and published economic and political data. It is a synthesis: of economic, political, and security aspects of West European developments and of factors internal and external to Western Europe.

This is a rewrite of the original report, which was drafted in the summer of 1995. It represents more than an ordinary update because much of what the original suggested might happen in the next four years, particularly in France, did in fact happen much more quickly—in the four months during which the report was being prepared to go to press.

The report is intended to be of use primarily to American decision-makers making policy with regard to the U.S. role in the North Atlantic Treaty Organization and U.S. relations to the European Union; secondarily to European decisionmakers.

The costs of the analysis, the travel, and the publication have been shared by RAND's Project AIR FORCE, Arroyo Center, National Defense Research Institute, International Policy Department, and European-American Center.

CONTENTS

FIGURE

TABLE

West European stability remains a vital interest of the United States; U.S. involvement in Western Europe remains a vital interest of Western Europe. Neither stability nor involvement, however, can be maintained simply by their recognition as vital interests. Foreign policy in democracies at peace is ordinarily dependent upon internal political considerations. Since the end of the Cold War, these considerations in Western Europe and the United States have been dominated by economic pressures, not all congruent with international interests perceived by foreign policy decisionmakers and commentators.

This report examines the potential economic, political, and security future of Western Europe as it passes the year 2000. It concludes that the region is currently stable and that stability is likely to continue but is by no means guaranteed. The major threat is economic. Unemployment throughout Western Europe is very high, in the 10-percent range. This has already brought about serious unrest in France, and a sharp cyclical downturn could lead to worse unrest, there and elsewhere.

The stable future that seems most likely is neither grim nor inspiring, but it is preferable to the dangers of instability. The policies of the United States and of the West European nations should stress avoidance of these dangers, in the economic and other realms, rather than the creation of speculative new futures.

The report looks first at the internal economic and political pressures in the three countries that dominate the European Union (EU) and the European portion of the North Atlantic Treaty Organization

(NATO): Germany, France, and the United Kingdom. It turns then to issues and institutional futures for EU and NATO. The results of these analyses are combined into a "canonical prediction" of the most likely state of Western Europe as it passes the millennium mark into 2000 through 2005. Since the one most certain thing about this canon is that it will not come to pass as predicted, optimistic and pessimistic variations are then examined. The report concludes with a discussion of policy implications for American and European decisionmakers.

THE EUROPEAN BIG THREE

Germany will continue to be dominated by the economics and politics of unification. The social problems of unification are being solved: Eastern Germany is beginning to look like western Germany; unemployment and related problems are being meliorated. This conceals a lot, however. Much of the employment in the east is subsidized, and no quick replacements have been found for the uneconomical heavy industries that dominated the German Democratic Republic. As a result, the costs of reconstruction continue to be heavy, and the Bundesbank has kept interest rates high to avoid inflation resulting from these costs. In early 1996, German unemployment moved above 10 percent, and the bank responded with modest cuts in interest rates but not enough to constitute any reversal of its tight-money anti-inflation policy.

Germany continues to be politically stable and is committed to continued EU integration centered on a European Monetary Union (EMU) with a single currency, albeit one that remains as conservatively managed as the deutsche mark is; continuation of NATO; expansion of both EU and NATO to the formerly communist states of Central Europe; and very careful participation in European and world security operations. The major political forces, the governing coalition led by the Christian Democratic Union and the Social Democratic opposition, agree to these principles. The major concrete threat is the possibility that the 1997 elections will lead to a coalition between the Social Democrats and the Greens, necessitating foreign-policy compromises with the radical views of the latter. Whatever the election outcome, however, Chancellor Kohl's successors in the new generation are unlikely to be as devoted to integration as he is.

Because the German economy dominates Europe, the Bundesbank's high interest rates reach across the entire continent. In Germany itself, the weight of these rates is balanced by the stimulus of reconstruction expenditures, but the rest of Western Europe bears the burden without the stimulus.

France is tied to Germany: politically and voluntarily because of the desire on both sides of the Rhine to prevent the recurrence of historical horrors; economically and slightly less voluntarily because of the dominance of the German economy and the Bundesbank. Largely as a result of the latter, French unemployment has stayed well above 10 percent in recent years, a fact that dominates French politics as well as economics. Since his election in May 1995, President Jacques Chirac and his Prime Minister, Alain Juppé, have tried to reduce unemployment by reforming the structural regulations, taxes, and impositions that are at the root of the high unemployment. Unfortunately, however, the dominance of the Bundesbank and the strong French desire to join the EMU have forced stringent fiscal and monetary policies that constrain growth and employment so tightly that the reforms can have no visible effect. The initial response to the Chirac-Juppé structural reforms was the strike-driven chaos of December 1995, and the government retreated on most fronts. France would benefit from a loosening of the tie to the deutsche mark, which would permit some devaluation of the franc and thus the combination of fiscal and monetary stimulus with structural reform. Although legitimate within the current European Monetary System, however, such devaluation would set back the drive toward the single currency.

The other critical French political problem, what to do about immigration and assimilation, particularly of Algerians and other Moslems, stems primarily from unemployment—the perception that immigrants compete with natives for jobs—although recent terrorist bombings have exacerbated it.

French economic malaise could cause problems even worse than December's if, rather than slowly improving or leveling off, unemployment were to increase further because of the business cycle or outside influences from Japan or the United States. A number of negative consequences would be possible. Most dangerous to France and to Europe would be major civil disturbances escalating from the December 1995 level to that of the 1968 student-worker demonstrations, which forced de Gaulle from power, and/or the rise of Jean-Marie Le Pen's radical right *Front National* to a position in which more moderate right-wing parties or populists would be tempted to bargain with him.

It is such possibilities, rather than nuclear testing or conflicts over Balkan policy, that might shake the current French devotion to a version of European integration somewhere between the German model of federation and the British desire for something that resembles General de Gaulle's *Europe des patries*. Events of this nature could also injure France's long-run grudging but solid adherence to NATO and the U.S. relationship, both of which have strengthened in recent years.

The United Kingdom is in many ways the most stable of the big three, even though its current government is the most likely to fall. The British economy has improved in recent years, partly because of former Prime Minister Thatcher's moves away from the regulations and other aspects of continental *dirigisme*, partly because of the devaluation of the pound made possible by Britain's said-to-be-temporary departure from the European Payments System. The desire to remain within Europe, but in its own traditional insular way, represents a British consensus. Prime Minister John Major is unpopular, and his Conservative Party is likely to lose the parliamentary elections due by 1997, but the Labour opposition is only marginally more pro-Europe. All sides are strongly pro-NATO, and although the "special relationship" with the United States has attenuated in recent years, it retains an inner core of great tensile strength.

THE EUROPEAN UNION

The future course of EU depends on three sets of developments.

Further economic integration—movement toward the EMU, with a single currency and a single central bank—is lagging. The initial 1997 target has already been postponed to the fallback date of 1999 set at Maastricht, and even that is becoming quite unrealistic. Establishment of EMU requires that a sufficient number of member states sign up and meet certain economic criteria, the most difficult of which concern deficits and budget discipline. EMU will require, de facto, the membership of Germany and either or both of Britain and France, and even Germany is currently failing to meet the criteria. The canonical prediction is that EMU will come into being, but not by 1999 and perhaps with less than a unique single currency and less than a fully powerful central bank. The question then will be whether delay will merely mean postponement, or whether it might induce a dangerous reverse trend away from European integration. And in any case, all bets are off if economic shocks injure the West European economy.

Political integration on security and other matters is not progressing rapidly on its own. Ad hoc arrangements, such as those between Britain and France in Yugoslavia, and symbolic institution-building, exemplified by the Eurocorps, are proceeding, but decisionmaking is not moving to Brussels or Strasbourg from national capitals. What might be more likely than any direct approach to political integration would be a series of events beginning with economic integration, particularly if and when an EMU with a single currency and a single central bank is in place. Such a bank would substitute EU control over monetary policy for any residual national control. That would in turn mean loss of national control over fiscal-budgetary policy. Budgets are inherently political, however, so that fiscal policy would be likely to be subject to some sort of joint decisionmaking mechanism, to preserve democracy. The resulting powerful EU institution might then extend its reach to security and other noneconomic matters, thus arriving at ultimate political integration. This is not a prediction, canonical or otherwise, for the next ten years. Rather, it is a suggestion that, if political integration is to come, it is more likely via the economic route than by Cartesian controversy or organizational manipulation.

Expansion of EU to Central European and other applicants is desired to strengthen the new democracies and tie them to the West, but such expansion will be slow and difficult at best. Bureaucratic obstacles built around the requirement for unanimity among current members mean that nothing is likely to happen before the turn of the millennium. Underlying are the explicit and implicit economic requirements for admission: free-market economies, economies strong enough to require little in the way of subsidies from existing EU members, and economies from which the free flow of goods will not do significant harm to competitive interests in existing member countries. These problems will be extremely difficult to overcome within any short period.

NATO

A Cold-War wisecrack-become-cliché about NATO summarized its objectives as: "To keep the Russians out, the Americans in, and the Germans down." The first and third of these are essentially obsolete, but "keeping the Americans in" Europe remains the vital function of the Alliance, agreed to on both sides of the Atlantic. This raises the first of three issues bearing on NATO's future.

Is NATO crumbling? Certainly, it is only a shadow of the mighty organization of the Cold War. The reduction in functions and forces has led to a feeling of malaise among those who had participated over the years. Nonetheless, large forces and structures do remain and show few signs of disappearing. Current concerns, however, focus more on crisis—failure to meet ongoing demands, particularly in Yugoslavia for a number of years—than on gradual crumbling. Paradoxically, NATO may in fact be in crisis, but not crumbling. Crises among the allies, particularly between the United States and European members, are not new. They came and went during the Cold War, and the Alliance remained sound, but the difference now is the loss of the counterbalancing Soviet threat. Even without that counterweight, however, sharp disagreements over Yugoslavia between the British and French on the one hand and the Americans on the other seem to have done little apparent damage to the fundamental relationship; the ease with which the three came back together in NATO's Bosnian campaign indicates that. One reason for the continuing solidity is a growing willingness, at least on the part of decisionmakers, to admit that the mutual vital interest in maintaining an American presence in Europe ought to suffice to justify the Alliance. It may not suffice, however, to maintain public support for substantial expenditures on a military alliance without a real military function, particularly in the United States.

One potential new mission for NATO is **expansion to the east** to shore up stability in the countries of Central Europe, particularly given the slow pace of their applications to EU. Their entry into NATO has already been agreed to in principle; the real questions concern when and how. This is a subject of disagreement, with one side advocating speed because of the need to maintain stability over the long time it will take EU to work its way, and the other cautioning about the negative effect on Russia of rapid NATO expansion. The fastest and most likely mode of entry into NATO, perhaps achievable by 2000, would be to admit at least the "Visegrad" states—Poland, the Czech Republic, Hungary, and perhaps Slovakia, which are deemed the most ready politically—to membership with concomitant Alliance guarantees against aggression, but without placing Western bases or stationed troops on their soil. Since the Russian military threat against which they would be guaranteed is practically nonexistent, admission without new bases would be relatively easy. It would be easy, however, because it would not be very real in contrast to admission to EU, which is slow because it involves strong economic interests.

To strengthen NATO, it would be useful to find **new military missions.** Expansion to Central Europe is not an example, because its purpose is as political and as empty of real military content as the existing function of keeping the Americans in. The Implementation Force effort in Bosnia may perhaps provide a prototype, however. Beyond that, individually improbable military missions, e.g., in the Middle East or a new threat from Russia or even China, might combine into a significant overall probability, but even that is questionable. New worldwide "clashes of civilizations" might renew a central mission for NATO; this seems even more unlikely. For the time being, the organization will have to subsist on its central political functions and a continuing search for additional military missions.

THE CANONICAL PREDICTION AND ALTERNATIVES

The **canonical prediction** coming out of these considerations is stability: economic and political stability within the West European states, stability of EU with modest progress toward economic and then political integration, and stability of NATO with possible growth to the east. This will be comfortable but not completely so, particularly if major military and human disturbances continue outside of the West; in any case, the more distant future appears less stable. Nonetheless, short-term stability will look preferable to instability.

Potential **economic variations** to the canon include, on the **optimistic** side, major reductions in unemployment rates, based either on spontaneous movements of the business cycle or conscious fiscal and monetary, as well as structural, policy; and accelerated economic integration of the EU. **Downside** variations include failure of monetary union and retarded economic integration of EU; political instability engendered by a failure to improve the unemployment picture; and the central danger to European stability, a significant economic downturn.

Optimistic security variations might be internal stabilization of Russia and its agreement to a partnership with a NATO that included former members of the Warsaw Pact, settling down of the Balkans, reduction of instability and threats in the Middle East and Maghreb, and successful attempts to reinvigorate NATO by restructuring the organization and its missions. **Pessimistic** possibilities include crumbling of NATO because of a failure to meet a critical threat; an unsuccessful attempt at restructuring; and a revival of American isolationism, perhaps stemming from either of the other two negative possibilities.

The dangers to the stable canon within this range of possible variations dominate the opportunities for improvement. These potential dangers seem more probable than the potential improvements, and their consequences more profound should they come to pass.

POLICY IMPLICATIONS

The central implication, both for the United States and Western Europe, is: Do no harm. Don't destabilize.

More specifically, for both sides of the Atlantic, the analysis implies preparation to act quickly against signs of economic downturn, readiness to assist Central Europe to grow economically toward the West, wariness about damaging NATO by trying to improve it, and alertness toward signs of serious out-of-area security threats.

For the United States, the central implication is the vital nature of continued participation in Europe and of taking care not to damage that relationship in the name of transitory moral or political objectives.

The major implications for the nations of Western Europe are the maintenance of EU as a vigorous ongoing organization, and wariness of damaging it by pushing political integration faster than can be supported by economics, or by putting it into false competition with NATO; the search for ways of improving the employment picture; and the resolution of the dilemma of demanding that the U.S. lead without being willing to follow.

ACKNOWLEDGMENTS

Very useful comments on earlier drafts were received from my RAND colleagues, Marten van Heuven (not the least of whose contributions was the suggestion that I amend my original title, which had Western Europe entering the second millennium), Robert Nurick, Gregory Treverton, and Kenneth Watman; from Martyn Piper and Bruno Tertrais, RAND research fellows from the British and French Ministries of Defense, respectively; and from Olivier Debouzy of the Paris law firm, August et Debouzy.

Chapter One

INTRODUCTION

> As a rule, democracies have very confused or erroneous ideas on external affairs, and generally solve outside questions only for internal reasons.
>
> —Alexis de Tocqueville

The focus of this analysis of alternative futures and policy responses is Western Europe: the European Union (EU) from County Galway to the *Land* of Brandenburg, and the European portion of the North Atlantic Treaty Organization (NATO) from the North Cape to Crete. Setting such a focus, however, does not imply either that this area can be treated as self-contained or that the issues of interest lie wholly within the area. Indeed, many of the crucial questions concern Western Europe's reaction to stimuli from the United States and from Russia, Eastern Europe, and Japan.

The policy issue for U.S. decisionmakers is how the state and status of Western Europe over the next decade, as it crosses the 2000 AD line, will affect American interests. A central premise is that West European stability remains a vital interest of the United States, as well as of the nation-states of Western Europe, and that U.S. involvement in Western Europe remains a vital interest of the West European states, as well as of the United States. These interests underlie the assumption that remains at the core of U.S. European policy: NATO is perhaps not the only possible vehicle for expression of joint American-European interests, but it has provided the institutional basis for maintaining them for nearly half a century, which suggests a strong presumption in favor of its continuation.

EU, however, must be treated more agnostically by an American. Secretary of State Warren Christopher has made clear that the United States

> supports Europe's integration and EU enlargement. . . [F]or our partnership to thrive, [it must take] specific steps in the economic and political arenas that will complement and reinforce our security relationship.[1]

But that implies no specific stand on the various issues of the speed and structure of European integration, and the devil is in the details.

In addition to these normative premises about American and European interests, one factual assumption, contained in the opening quotation from de Tocqueville, also underlies the analysis: National policies are driven by internal political considerations. Added here is that, at this time in history, particularly since the end of the Cold War, internal politics are in turn driven largely by economics. To be sure, other pressures may arise, e.g., security threats or ideological challenges strong enough to cause nations to subordinate their primary economic interests. No such threats or challenges are now visible on the European-American horizon, however, although some are certainly possible. Lacking such major threats, security policies will be outcomes rather than inputs, as will organizational changes and what has been termed the "poetry" of policymaking, somewhere between organization and ideology—the historical U.S.-British "special relationship," for example. Organizational restructuring and poetry may help shape outcomes but is unlikely to direct them.

The analysis will set forth a "most likely" prediction, a canonical future, but since any such prediction is inherently of very low probability in itself, a range of possible alternatives will also be explored. The canonical prediction for Western Europe is the one implied by the title of this report[2]: The most likely course will be undramatic—gradual economic followed by political integration, gradual expansion of

---

[1]Warren Christopher, "Charting a Transatlantic Agenda for the 21st Century," address, Madrid, June 2, 1995.

[2]"Not with a bang but a whimper" is the last line of T. S. Eliot's poem, "The Hollow Men."

West European institutions to Central Europe, and modest economic growth. All this will be very slow, much slower than most advocates of integration hope. Even by 2005, few political, economic, or security configurations drastically different from those of 1995 will have appeared.

In addition to not-now-predictable security stresses, however, such an outcome could be defeated by its own feedback. Too slow economic progress, in particular, bringing about little improvement in current high levels of unemployment in Western Europe while at the same time increasing the already heavy burdens placed on European economies by social welfare expenditures, could produce strong political dissent. Therefore, one important potential variation from the canonical outcome is that economic dissatisfaction might produce internal stress and thus radical external, as well as internal, change. Indeed, the greatest threat to the benign stability of the canonical outcome would be a European economy in which progress is not merely too slow but has reversed into a dangerous downturn.

Encouraging the stable canonical outcome and avoiding stress-based variations ought to be the central objective of European and Atlantic policy for both the United States and the nation-states of Western Europe. The canonical outcome is not inspiring; whimpers are not, but they may be preferable to ambitious bangs.

The structure of the discussion stems from the factual and normative premises:

- The initial discussion will be of the three central decisionmaking states of Western Europe: Germany, France, and the United Kingdom. The smaller members of EU and NATO are not trivial, but their decisions largely concern whose coalition to join on what issues. (Italy is large enough and rich enough to convert the Big Three into the Big Four, but until it gets its internal politics together—which may be never—it is unlikely to be a primary player. Spain is also growing up—with multiple growing pains.)

- This will lead to an analysis of the political economy of Western Europe as a whole: the path toward further economic integration—the European Monetary Union (EMU) and the single currency; the parallel route toward integration of political decisionmaking, particularly on security and other foreign policy; and the enlargement of EU by the accession of central European states.

- From political economy and EU, the discussion will turn to security matters and NATO, including the issues of the potential crumbling of NATO as the result of recurring post–Cold War crises; the expansion of NATO into central Europe in parallel (or not) to the expansion of EU; and possible new military missions for the Alliance.

- These segments having mapped out the canonical outcome, the final "predictive" section will examine a range of alternative "what-if?" variations.

- The story will conclude with a discussion of the implications for current and near-term policy, both for the United States and the nations of Western Europe.

Chapter Two

THE BIG THREE

GERMANY

Since the fall of the Wall in November 1989, the central issue structuring German economic, social, and political policies and outcomes has been the need to achieve real integration of the former German Democratic Republic (GDR)—East Germany—into the Federal Republic of Germany.

Initial political euphoria led to the widespread belief in the Federal Republic that the powerful West German economy could correct the economic deficiencies of the East in a matter of a few years and with few difficulties. Even though many German economists and businessmen saw the July 1990 replacement of the weak East German *ostmark* by the powerful deutsche mark at parity between the two as an economic mistake, they realized the compelling social and political reasons for bringing the East Germans quickly into the West, and they felt that the error would throw up no more than a minor obstacle to integration.

To many non-German economists, however, this belief appeared overoptimistic on the problems and the timing of integration, and in fact it has proven to be so. Two years later, Charles Cooper and I noted that:

> The transition from Communist to productive market economies is proving far harder, more costly, and more time consuming to bring about than expected. . . . Let us make clear, however, that we do not view Germany's economic problem primarily as a failure of policy.

> ... True, the dreadful ... gap between East and West German
> productivity was woefully underestimated; and some of the
> political/economic decisions made in 1990 were, in retrospect,
> jumps that carried half of the way across a wide chasm.
> Nonetheless, the chasm is there and nobody has figured out how to
> cross it. The chasm lies between: on the one hand, the economic
> difficulties of equalizing productivity between the 1990 economy
> and one firmly based on the Stalinist shibboleths of the 1940s; and
> on the other hand, the social intolerability of leaving one part of a
> nation to gradually climb out of a 1945 standard of living, while the
> other part progresses into the 21st century. Such a chasm would
> exist even if the ostmark had been converted at 5:1.[1]

Since 1992, Germany has neither jumped across the chasm, nor, fortunately, has it jumped part of the way and thus fallen into social
chaos. Rather, the Germans have moved sensibly toward closing the
gap between social needs and economic realities. Closure has pro-
gressed more readily in the realm of avoiding the intolerability of
drastically unequal standards of living—that was what *ostmark–
deutsche mark* parity was all about—than in the realm of equalizing
productivity. As a result, Germany today is socially and politically
stable but carries a heavy economic burden. And because the
German economy remains the flywheel of economic activity
throughout EU, the burden extends to all of Western Europe, domi-
nating the political, as well as the economic, transition to the next
millennium.

The day-to-day visible face of eastern Germany has improved im-
measurably. In 1990 and 1991, an observer dropped into Germany,
urban or rural, would have had no difficulty figuring out which half
of that recently divided land he was in. The West was lively and vital
in the prosperous German version of a Western Europe that had
been developing democratically and economically for 45 years; this
could be seen in the homes, the stores, the automobiles, the facto-
ries, the lights, the publications, and the faces. East Germany remained drab, just coming to life politically and socially, unproduc-

---

[1]Charles Cooper and Robert Levine, "The United States and Germany in the World
Economy," in Heiner Flassbeck, Wolfgang Gerstenberger, Charles Cooper, Robert
Levine, *The RAND/DIW/IFO Conference on the European Challenge and the Role of the
USA*, Santa Monica, Calif.: RAND, CF-107-RC, 1993, p. 55.

tive and poverty-stricken. Change had begun most visibly in Berlin, but the condition of East Berlin in 1991 was exemplified by the fact that a new hotel fully up to western standards (and prices) had only one phone line connecting it to West Berlin and the rest of the world.

In 1995, Berlin moved toward again becoming the center of gravity of Germany, and East Berlin moved again toward becoming the center of gravity of Berlin. The local bird is the building crane; museums and parks, and now federal government buildings, are being restored to their former glory. The best theater and opera, and some of the best restaurants, are in the East. Even more significant, however, residential and shopping streets in the East look a lot like those in the West; apartment fronts are a little shabbier, autos a little older (but they are VWs, not Trabis); even so, the homes, shops, and people look very similar. Less frequently commented on but at least as important, similar observations can be made in many parts of the rest of the former GDR. The towns and the shops and the weekly markets look like those in West Germany. The fields are lush, and houses are being built in the towns and the countryside. It is difficult to tell when one is crossing the former "inter-German border."

These visible changes in eastern Germany are very striking. They illustrate the increasing social equalization, but to a great extent they are on the surface, concealing many continuing problems. For one thing, the *Ossis* and the *Wessis*, East and West Germans, are still very different. To oversimplify, many *Ossis* feel that the *Wessis* patronize them at best, treating them as recent entrants into capitalist civilization who must be educated into substituting risk-taking for guaranteed security. Many *Wessis* feel that is exactly how *Ossis* must be treated. The *weltanschauungs* and political attitudes on the two sides of the former border differ sharply. This was documented by opinion surveys designed by Ronald Asmus soon after the fall of the Wall[2]; it is still reflected in electoral results that are significantly further to the left in the old East. And the prosperity and the new "westernness" of the East are in part carried there by westerners— entrepreneurs, officials, vacationers. Many of the new homes, for example, are occupied by *Wessis*, others by the small minority of *Ossis*

---

[2]Ronald D. Asmus, *German Strategy and Opinion After the Wall 1990–1993*, Santa Monica, Calif.: RAND, MR-444-FNF/OSD/A/AF, 1994, provides the most recent summary.

who have gained new jobs with federal or state governments or with western firms. This illustrates the continuing underlying problem, the economic one.

The residents of eastern Germany can be divided into three groups: those westerners and easterners who have integrated into the German capitalist economy, easterners who are not suffering much economically because of various government subsidies, and those who are still doing poorly. The subsidized middle group is much the largest. Some of their subsidies are payments for real work for real needs. Construction of public infrastructure is a major portion of the needed reconstruction of the East. East German autobahns, for example, like all other European and American superhighways, are subject to annoying delays for repairs, but in the East, the obstacles seem to come every ten or twenty kilometers. For anyone who drove in the East soon after the Wall came down, the need for such public works was obvious, but economically they provide only a transitional bridge to an eastern economy integrated into the West—and the bridge will have to be a long one. And many of the subsidies have much weaker economic foundations—make-work jobs that are partially subsidized to compensate for continuing productivity differences, or just plain social safety nets.

The fact is that the East German economy still has a very long way to go to catch up with the West. The percentage rate of growth in the East is much more rapid than that in the West, but that is because it has started from a base that was relatively low when Germany was divided and became much lower after unification, when much of the communist industrial garbage was thrown out or allowed to crumble. The construction sector in the East, private as well as public, is booming (but construction booms are inherently transitory); retail and wholesale trade took off quickly after currency unification imposed western levels of consumer demand on a communist distribution system; and various manufacturing subsectors are doing nicely. Nonetheless, the problem of how to compensate for the mid-twentieth-century heavy industries—chemicals, steel, etc.—that dominated the economy of the GDR and achieved instant obsolescence on the day of unification has not been solved.

That problem and related ones will be solved, but it will take a lot more time and a lot more subsidies. In the meantime, however, the worst *social* fears of 1990 and 1991 have been alleviated. Germany is one nation-state. True, *Ossis* and *Wessis* are in substantially different economic circumstances and have substantially different views, politically and otherwise. But to draw a U.S. analogy, the differences are no greater than those between the American North and the American South for a full century after the Civil War. As in the United States, the constitutional question has been answered; Germany is a single federal state, and all differences will be worked out politically. Indeed, pursuing the U.S. analogy even further, the several *Länder* of the former GDR are beginning to provide different seedbeds for economic development—Brandenburg, for example, has done better in solving the legal questions of land tenure after the succession of Nazi and Communist regimes than has Lower Saxony—but the differences are no greater than those between North Carolina and Mississippi.

As one result of this partial but sufficient social and political unification, no direct political line can be drawn from unification or remaining regionalism to Germany's external policies and attitudes. Indeed, the Nazi past still resonates through German foreign policy more strongly than does the communist past. Asmus suggests, for example, that German willingness to participate in NATO or other international military peacekeeping is developing gradually under a series of political constraints, constraints whose roots go back to the World War II depredations of German troops throughout Europe.

The opposition Social Democratic Party (SPD) favors more limitations than does Chancellor Helmut Kohl's Christian Democratic Union (CDU)-led governing coalition, but enough Social Democrats favor German participation that the constrained movement toward peacekeeping participation would be likely to continue even if an SPD-led government were to replace the CDU after the next election, in 1997. This is particularly true because of what Asmus calls "the desire by German political leaders to prevent Bundeswehr missions from becoming partisan and polarizing issues in German politics."[3] True, a change in direction could possibly stem from the formation of a coalition government joining the SPD to the radical Green party

---

[3]Ronald D. Asmus, *Germany's Contribution to Peacekeeping: Issues and Outlook*, Santa Monica, Calif.: RAND, MR-602-OSD, 1995, p. 46.

after the election. (Such coalitions currently govern several *Länder*.) That seems unlikely, but it is by no means impossible, particularly if Germany suffers economic difficulties.

On a more general and more important issue, Germany's policies toward EU seem similarly determined by a broad political consensus. Politically, Germans want progress toward tighter European integration; some dare use the term "federation," some not, but that is a question of speed and of rhetoric. Karl Lammers, a spokesman on Europe for the CDU, has advocated movement toward a true federation, but it was made clear that this was a personal, not a party or government, position. In any case, most Germans seem to favor movement toward a single European currency—but one that looks and acts a lot like the deutsche mark. They are in no hurry, however; some argue that an unsatisfactory compromise resulting in a new currency even slightly weaker than the deutsche mark would be unacceptable.

Germany also favors inclusion of the former Communist countries of central Europe—particularly the Czech Republic, Poland, and Hungary—in EU and NATO, again with differences over speed.

The tone of Germany's positions on these issues has for many years been set by Chancellor Kohl, much the most European among EU's major national leaders and among the most European in Germany. When he departs, the next government of whatever party will be led by younger politicians who feel less overhang of the Nazi past. This makes compromise to achieve integration less urgent to the newer leaders, although paradoxically that is due in large measure to the unquestioned assumption that the new Germany exists as an organic and inalienable part of Western Europe. If the Bundesbank controls Europe's economy now, and does so prudently and properly, why share power over a substitute, single European currency?

The politics of unification has little to do with these issues of German external policy, but the economics of unification and reconstruction is central to them and to almost all other German issues. That is because the subsidy and other costs of unification are so large as to provide both direction and major constraints for the Federal German budget and thus for the economy. From 1991 to 1995, the flow of public funds from West to East Germany has been estimated at about one trillion deutsche marks (more than $700 billion at 1995 exchange rates, more when most of it was spent).[4] Although the figures and concepts are not completely comparable, this is around 7.5 percent of German GDP. To calibrate that number for Americans, the U.S. defense budget is about 4 percent of GDP.

Such an immense sum constrains German budgetary and monetary policy. It leaves little room for expansion of social or other expenditures; financed in part by increased taxes, it engenders the usual and universal sour effect that high taxes impose on politics in democratic states. Because of the historic German fear of inflation, it constrains wage bargains, thus exacerbating labor-management conflicts and leaving both sides grumbling. And more important, to prevent unification-induced inflation, the Bundesbank has maintained a tight-money, high-interest-rate policy during the five years since currency unification, thus inhibiting economic growth. Together with the stultifying labor-market and other rigid regulations that are endemic throughout the continent, it has kept unemployment high in both western and eastern Germany.

As discussed in the next section, French economic rigidities combined with monetary and fiscal tightness have induced a chronically high rate of unemployment and consequent social and political disturbances. This has not yet happened in Germany, but it may well be on the way. By early 1996, the Bundesbank was cutting interest rates in response to the rise in all-German rates to above 10 percent, but the moves were far from dramatic, and inflationary fears still dominated.

The effects of Bundesbank enactments, while dependent on German economic conditions, however, are not confined to Germany. The power of the German economy is such that Bundesbank monetary policy constrains and controls economic activity throughout Western Europe. As a result, *the costs of German unification, acting on and through Bundesbank monetary policy, have inhibited growth and kept unemployment high throughout Western Europe. Because the costs are not decreasing, this constraint continues to be the single most important economic factor governing Western Europe's transition to*

---

[4] *This Week in Germany*, June 23, 1995, cites that estimate from the *Suddeutsche Zeitung*.

the third millennium; because of the effect of economics on politics, it is probably also the single most important political factor.

FRANCE

The country tied most closely to Germany, politically and economically, is France. The word "couple" is frequently used to describe the two, and it is not meant ironically.

True, the two nations remain separate and in some ways very different, with the French and Germans sometimes looking askance at what they see as the collective and historical characteristics of the other. (The "houses of horrors" at some French carnivals, for example, still have among the terrors painted on the front a World War I *boche* in a spiked helmet.) Nonetheless, such traditional differences are no deeper than those between other European nations that cherish their uniqueness and remember their histories—France and Britain, Britain and Germany, even Norway and Denmark, for example—and they no longer have very much to do with real ongoing political or economic relationships. A large mainstream consensus in both France and Germany upholds the close ties between the two, as insurance that centuries of warfare have come to an end and that Nazism is buried with a stake through its heart.

This political coupling has made possible, and is in turn strongly supported by, increasingly close economic ties. Since German unification, however, the closeness has led to increasing economic problems for France. The economies of the two are closely intertwined; since Germany is the larger and the stronger, the monetary policies of the Bundesbank govern the French economy, as well as the German.

Because the Bundesbank has seen as its major task since 1990 the controlling of the inflationary pressures stemming from reconstruction spending, the effects of its monetary constraints have extended to France, as well as to Germany. For France, however, they have been even more constraining. German monetary tightness has been compensated to a substantial extent by the Keynesian fiscal stimulus inherent in the increased public and private spending for reconstruction; indeed, that is the reason for the Bundesbank's tight policies. France, however, has suffered from the tightness without benefiting from the stimulus. The French unemployment rate rose from 8.9 percent in 1990 to a peak of 12.4 percent in 1994; it dropped slightly by mid-1995, but was still well above 10 percent. In early 1996, it began to increase again. West German unemployment, which had been somewhat lower than the French for many years in any case, rose less, and began to drop a year earlier; in 1994 it was 8.3 percent, four points below the French rate, although it too began to rise in 1996.[5]

Unemployment in general, and two categories in particular—long-term unemployment and the job-finding difficulties of youths just entering the labor force—are central to French politics. Dissatisfaction with the 14 years of experience under President François Mitterrand and the two years under Prime Minister and presidential candidate Edouard Balladur was a major factor in Jacques Chirac's defeat of Balladur and Lionel Jospin, the candidate of Mitterrand's Socialist Party, in the 1995 presidential elections. Chirac promised to make the reduction of unemployment his central goal. What happened after that, culminating in the strikes and demonstrations at the end of 1995, illustrated the great difficulties in bringing about any substantial improvement.

French (like all) unemployment has two causes: macroeconomic, having to do with the condition and growth rate of the aggregate economy, and microeconomic, having to do with the internal structure of the economy. Neither macroeconomic nor microeconomic remedies for unemployment are likely to work very well without complementary remedies on the other side. Macroeconomically, the growth rate must be sufficient to create more new jobs than there are job seekers; microeconomically, employers must not see the new jobs as being so encumbered by regulations, costs, and risks as to be afraid to fill them. Chirac and Alain Juppé, his Prime Minister, have not been able or willing to do enough on either economic front.

On the macroeconomic side, to accelerate French growth sufficiently to create the needed jobs, either the Bundesbank must weaken its priority on fighting inflation at the cost of growth, or France must somehow loosen the tie to Germany and the bank without breaking

---

[5]The economic situations of West and East Germany are so different that many data series are still kept separate.

it. Almost nobody wants to rebuild barriers within Europe, although Nobel Laureate economist Maurice Allais, who advocates EU protectionism to reduce unemployment, comes close to espousing French protection in the meantime. In mid-1995, he wrote that "In the present situation of the European Union, which is dominated by great confusion, France must guard fully all decision possibilities."[6]

Allais is considered extreme, however, and in any case the French and German economies are too closely connected to be separated very far. Rather, what could be done, legitimately and within current rules, would be for the French to cut interest rates while allowing the franc to float relative to the deutsche mark within the 15-percent range allowed by a 1992 decision of the European Monetary System (EMS). That would lead to a de facto partial devaluation of the franc, which would in turn increase French export prospects, while permitting interest rates to drop and allowing room for stimulative fiscal policies. It is notable that Britain, which left the European Payments System (EPS) and allowed the pound to float and thus effectively devalue itself in September 1992, reduced its unemployment rate from 10 percent in that year—0.4 points less than France's—to 8.3 percent in mid-1995, 3.3 points less than France's.

For reasons both political and ideological, this is not likely to happen in France, however. Even in the depths of the December 1995 chaos, devaluation was not considered as an option. The long-standing policy of *le franc fort*, the strong franc, apparently remains solid. The policy has been based both on the need to disown earlier periods of monetary and budgetary irresponsibility and on the desire to keep France tightly tied to EU in general and Germany in particular. Since the Maastricht agreement of 1991, the economic aspect of this effort has focused on the need for France to enter and remain within the strict monetary and fiscal requirements for joining the future single-currency–based European Monetary Union (EMU) (not to be confused with the existing EMS, the European Monetary System), scheduled to begin no later than 1999.

---

[6]Maurice Allais, "Le chômage et l'ordre public: Une indepensable et urgente protection communitaire [Unemployment and Public Order: Indispensable and urgent [community protection]," *Le Figaro*, June 13, 1995, p. 2.

These are excellent reasons for maintaining *le franc fort*, and nobody advocates abandoning it completely. French economist Pierre Jacquet, however, suggests redefining it:

> [It is not] necessary to renounce the objective of "strong," or rather, stable money. But, just as the force of the mark is not defined by the objective of a rate of exchange to be defended in detail against the outside, that of the franc should be tied to the intrinsic virtues of our economic policy and not to the objective of exchange. . . . [This] implies . . . making flexible the objective of franc-mark exchange. Would that not be a minimal "price" to pay for the preservation of three other even more important objectives: that of maintaining price stability, that of reducing public deficits, and that of creating macroeconomic conditions more propitious for the creation of jobs?[7]

His phrase "'strong' or rather stable money" emphasizes the French consensus on the need for *le franc stable*. Its transmutation into *le franc fort*, however, seems additionally to imply a set level with regard to the deutsche mark in particular, an implication he questions.

So far, however, the Chirac-Juppé government has shown no sign of moving away from *le franc fort* as currently defined in terms of exchange rates. The politics of doing so would be difficult, particularly because of the ideology, widely shared throughout the developed world, that the sole purpose of monetary policy is to combat inflation. In France, this is powerfully represented by Jean-Claude Trichet, the Governor of the Banque de France, which as a step toward the single currency has recently been given the independence from governmental policy required by Maastricht.

For those reasons, in the autumn of 1995, Chirac and Juppé tried to start out on a purely microeconomic course toward unemployment reduction. The proposals Juppé presented to the Parliament and the nation, however, had macroeconomic implications, as well as microeconomic, and the macroeconomic effects were perverse in regard to growth and employment. To move toward the Maastricht criteria, taxes were raised and social benefits cut, thereby constraining rather than stimulating the economy.

---

[7] Pierre Jacquet, in "Enjeux," *Les Echos*, July 1995.

In any case, the difficulties of microeconomic measures to reduce French unemployment are at least as great as those on the macroeconomic side. France's existing problems are overregulation; overtaxing, particularly of payrolls; too high a "safety net"; and overstructuring of the economy by the government. Together, these make it difficult and costly for employers to hire and difficult and costly to fire, which further inhibits the initial hiring; on the other side, it leaves the unemployed comfortable enough in that status that they have insufficient incentive to go out and look for jobs. This is true throughout Western Europe, but it is more acute in France than in any of the other large economies. (It is much less true in the United States, as a result of which U.S. unemployment rates have been much lower than European in recent years, but U.S. income inequality and insecurity have become much greater. There are no very satisfactory answers.)

Most French economists and members of the political class agree in general about what should be done: Reduce regulations; reduce payroll taxes; reduce unemployment benefits; reduce employment in the public sector; and reduce *dirigisme*, government management of the economic structure.

Cutting benefits is never politically popular, however. Neither is changing the kinds of regulations relevant here, e.g., those making firing costly, those that mandate long paid vacations. Perhaps the French would be willing to trade off some of their benefits in favor of significantly lower unemployment, but microeconomic structural changes of the type called for would take a long time to work their favorable effects, and the results would be uncertain at best. In the meantime, the costs to those whose benefits were reduced would be imposed immediately. This would cause political difficulty at any time, and extreme difficulty when unemployment is high. One possible way out would be to use macroeconomic measures to cut unemployment while introducing deregulation and benefit cuts, but as discussed above, that has been ruled out.

Nonetheless, Chirac and Juppé tried the microeconomic-only route, with results that should have been predictable.[8] In November 1995,

---

[8]They were predicted in an earlier draft of this report, but to happen over a period of years, not months.

Prime Minister Juppé announced to the National Assembly a series of measures involving closing the social security deficit, raising some taxes, reducing various benefits, and reducing the pension rights of various public employees, particularly those in the French railroad system. Led by the rail unions, many workers, including those in the Paris subways, went out on strike. Transport was frozen; Paris was almost frozen as people went to jobs by foot, by bicycle, by boat, and by traffic jam. In spite of the inconvenience and the fact that the rail workers at the center of the strike were insisting on the preservation of special benefits not available to anyone else and going back more than 100 years, a majority of the French sided with the strikers.

By Christmas, the government had folded on most of the key substantive issues, although it preserved some changes in the process that may provide it with more flexibility in the future. The strikes ground to an exhausted halt without solving any of the fundamental structural problems. Meanwhile, unemployment turned upward, largely for macroeconomic reasons. Now, further increases, even minor ones, will exacerbate all problems; a major recession starting from a 10–12 percent unemployment rate would be devastating. Such a failure to achieve any significant reduction in unemployment could have a strong effect on the other major political issue, immigration.

Although the perception of immigrants competing with natives for scarce jobs is central to fear of immigration among the metropolitan French, the opposition has several other bases as well. One, of course, is pure racism, although that has never been strong in France. Closely allied, however, is the fear of a failure of the large number of Arabs from Algeria and other parts of the Maghreb to assimilate into French culture as have past immigrants. All nations that welcome or accept immigrants desire their assimilation, but in contrast to the United States, where the culture has historically adapted to new immigrant groups as the immigrants adapted to the culture, France (and other European nations) insist on assimilation in which almost all the changes are made by the immigrants. Some French sociologists believe that such assimilation is taking place among the second-generation Maghrebians, but that view is not widespread.

Another basis for anti-immigration views is the endemic violence, drug use, etc., among youth in the suburbs, which have become the French equivalent of American central cities, because that is where the public housing has been built. The 1995 movie, *La Haine* (The Hatred), which was considered very important by many in the French political class, suggested subtly that suburban social conflicts are based much more on generation, class, and unemployment than on ethnicity, but this is not yet obvious to most of the French. On the other hand, with the Algerian civil war apparently lapping over into France, as marked by the bombings that began in the summer of 1995, the fear of failed assimilation may strengthen.

Withal, the key factors accelerating anti-immigration views in the mid-1990s are high unemployment and economic insecurity, and the consequent belief that "they are taking our jobs."

Continued high unemployment and its anti-immigration offspring may have strong political effects in one or more of several directions. A major increase in unemployment would almost certainly have such effects, of which the 1995 disturbances were a precursor.

The least traumatic effect would be **sharp reduction or even reversal of the government majority in the Chamber of Deputies.**   The French electoral schedule is an unusual one, with presidential and legislative elections taking place on independent timetables. As a result, Socialist President Mitterrand served his last two years with an 80-percent center-right majority in the Chamber and was thereby forced into *cohabitation* with a Gaullist prime minister, Balladur. Happily for Mitterrand's successor, Chirac, he inherited the same majority.   With the next legislative elections scheduled for 1998, however, continued high unemployment would be likely to reduce this majority and perhaps even reverse it, just as the left majority that followed Mitterrand's 1988 reelection was reversed in the 1993 election of the current Chamber. To be sure, should such a reversal seem likely going into 1998, Chirac might well replace Juppé, perhaps with Philippe Seguin, the nationalistic and relatively anti-European president of the Chamber of Deputies, or Charles Pasqua, Balladur's tough Interior Minister. Either of them would be more likely to de-emphasize EMU and *le franc fort* in favor of macroeconomic stimulus for French employment. It is doubtful, however, that a change of prime ministers could have an early enough economic effect to prevent a 1998 political turnaround if that were in the cards.

A turnaround in 1998 would end the center-right government and force President Chirac into *cohabitation* with a leftist prime minister. *Cohabitation* worked badly in the 1980s when Mitterrand was an active president and Chirac his active prime minister; it worked better in the 1990s with an aging Mitterrand and a gentler Prime Minister Balladur. Going into the 2000s with an active President Chirac tied to an opposing prime minister could be a formula for immobilism and further deterioration with regard to the problems that had brought about the hypothesized 1998 political reversal.

A political shift within the ongoing right-left cycle of the Fifth Republic would pose no immediate structural problems, although *cohabitation* and immobilism would likely lead to postponement and exacerbation. A Parisian journalist warns of worse, however: "a society in decline, with the resurgence of old demons and demagogues of all types."[9] These could be manifest in two ways:

Increases in unemployment or failure to make significant improvements could bring about major unrest worse than that of the fall of 1995. Such unrest has occurred in France with some historical frequency. The most recent occasion was in 1968, when students and then some workers took to the streets, causing chaos for several weeks and ultimately the final political withdrawal of General de Gaulle. Ten years earlier, the rise of de Gaulle and the Fifth Republic took place by extra-constitutional means in an atmosphere of unrest; that was followed by several years in which a revolution against de Gaulle, led by French generals in Algeria, was mounted and suppressed. Twenty years before that, continuing depression-and-unemployment-based social and political polarization played a major role in weakening the Third Republic and thus facilitating its defeat by the Third Reich; this was followed by the years of Vichy. And so forth, back to 1789.

In December 1994, not many French took the possibility of a recurrence of such unrest very seriously; by December 1995, many more did. If unemployment is not reduced significantly, and certainly if it

---

[9]Jacques Jublin, *La Tribune*, September 6, 1995.

rises significantly without having been reduced in the interim, the possibilities may become substantially greater.

At least as worrisome, **the influence of Jean-Marie Le Pen's extreme-right *Front National* could increase sharply.** Making his racist view of immigration his central plank, Le Pen did well in the first round (anybody can play) of the 1995 presidential elections, achieving in excess of 15 percent, a small increase over his showing seven years earlier. Seen as more ominous by French political commentators, however, the *Front* increased its influence in the municipal elections that followed the presidential vote by a month. Municipal elections in France are quite important politically, providing the basis for regional and ultimately national political power. For the first time, the *Front National* elected the mayors of a number of major and minor cities, led by Toulon, the fifth largest in France. Since then, Le Pen has attempted to take advantage of the late-1995 chaos and has even extended his mischief internationally by making common cause with the Russian Fascist, Vladimir Zhirinovsky. Increasing dissatisfaction with the Chirac-Juppé government because of failure to cope with unemployment could strengthen the *Front National* further. It is unlikely to approach anywhere near a majority; after a brief post–World-War-II period when association with Vichy made anything on the right questionable, at least 10 percent of the French electorate has always been on the far right, but never more than 20 percent. An April 1996 survey, however, indicated that 28 percent of the respondents were "responsive" to Le Pen's ideas, a substantial increase over 19 percent a year earlier. Such a change, attributable largely to growing economic woes, may tempt other parties, either of the moderate right and center or the populist left, to bargain with him rather than treat him as the pariah he now is. The French electoral system gave the *Front* no seats in the Chamber in the last election, but that could change dramatically.

Under de Gaulle's constitution of the Fifth Republic, the president, not the prime minister, retains responsibility for foreign policy and defense. As first president of the new republic, de Gaulle used his strong and prickly foreign policies to establish external independence as a major support for internal *amour-propre* and unity after the Algerian-revolt–based disunity of the 1950s. This has been the basis of the famous French foreign-policy consensus.

The consensus continued after de Gaulle's departure in 1969 and up until the present; domestic difficulties have caused few reciprocal reactions back into foreign policy areas, except on economic matters related to EMU. Chirac's refusal to back off on nuclear testing in the South Pacific, even though it reduced his immediate personal popularity in French public opinion polls, helped preserve an image of international strength. His initiation of proposals for military defense of the United Nations' remaining "safe havens" for Bosnians, his enthusiastic endorsement of the NATO operations that did take place, and his willingness to use French forces for those purposes have also contributed to the strong image.

More recently, Chirac and the government have proposed a radical reduction and revamping of France's armed forces. The proposals include such emotional matters as abandoning bases in historical garrison towns and ending compulsory national military service, which has been traditionally considered a key support for national unity and indeed *Fraternité*. They notably exclude reduction of France's contribution to the Eurocorps, the joint military organization composed of French, German, and other West European units.

Chirac's proposals are controversial and will be extensively debated, but not even they, let alone nuclear testing and Yugoslavia, are likely to play a major role as compared to unemployment and immigration in determining France's political future. Foreign and defense policies are outputs, not inputs.

With the exception of nuclear testing—and so far as France is concerned, that is a minor issue destined to become more minor when France signs a permanent test ban treaty—foreign policy has changed little with the accession of Chirac. France still mildly espouses the gradual extension of NATO to the central European states; and the Chirac-Juppé government continues to favor continued political, as well as economic, integration of EU, but with an objective somewhere between German desires for rapid federation and British reluctance to integrate Europe any further. Part of the French dilemma is a general desire to move toward the single currency, balanced by a strong reluctance to submerge political independence in a European federation. For most of the French, de Gaulle's *Europe des patries* is still the political if no longer the economic ideal.

On a shorter time horizon, France has been finding more common ground with Britain than in the past. The French would like to move closer to the UK to slow down the German move toward European federalism but to do so without getting too close to the United States, which is still viewed as having a "special relationship" with the British. The common French-British experience in Yugoslavia has helped here, and the long-standing cultural barriers between the French and British military leaderships are beginning to break down. Nonetheless, Seguin, the president of the Chamber of Deputies, has claimed that the worldwide anti-nuclear-testing protests were an Anglo-Saxon conspiracy. For a while, various joint military procurement possibilities had been seen as helping move the French and the British together, but the British choice of the American Apache helicopter over a French competitor did not help this. In any case, the Channel is still very wide. Neither can one yet wade across the Rhine.

The Atlantic Ocean is also very wide, but it is not getting wider. French irritations at what they saw as American gyrations, inconsistencies, partisanship, and underhandedness with regard to Yugoslavia were very real but not very deep. The 1995 controversy over mutual industrial espionage showed some of the same characteristics. On the other hand, France's 1996 move to participate in NATO's military structure without formally rejoining it was a less dramatic move than it might have seemed; the French had been participating de facto, as necessary, all along.

The fundamental French attitude toward the United States and NATO has remained constant for many years. It is based primarily on the recognition that Britain is not a sufficient balance for Germany, and the U.S. presence in Europe through NATO remains an essential counterweight to German dominance of the continent.[10] French officials have long extended private assurances to the effect that France would be there when needed to any American who would listen. They still are.

Much remains to be played out in France. But à la de Tocqueville, any major changes are far more likely to come from internal pres-

---

[10]See Robert A. Levine, *France and the World: A Snapshot at Mid-Decade*, Santa Monica, Calif.: RAND, P-7901, 1995, pp. 10–14.

sures stemming from economics, unemployment, and immigration than from external events.

THE UNITED KINGDOM

The economy of the United Kingdom is less tightly tied to Germany's than is that of France, and at least in the most recent years, the British have benefited from that relative looseness. Figure 1 shows West German, French, and British unemployment rates from 1979 through 1994. The chart has several interesting aspects. First, the three economies show similar cyclical patterns. That is to be expected; the economies of the developed world have moved together since the Great Depression, and the U.S. pattern in the 1980s and

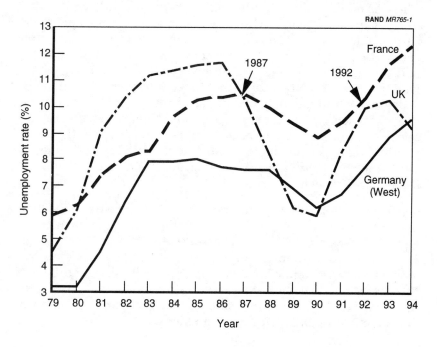

SOURCE; OECD, *OECD Economic Outlook*, Paris, June 1995, Annex Table 22.

Figure 1—Standardized Unemployment Rates: France, UK, and West Germany

1990s has differed little from the European experience illustrated by the figure.

Second, however, Britain, which had been performing much more poorly than its two partners in the first half of the 1980s, began to improve in the middle of the decade. It does not take too much of a leap of faith to attribute that, at least in part, to Prime Minister Margaret Thatcher's loosening of many of the structural binds on British economic activity as she moved toward an unconstrained free-market model. (But as in the United States, decreased unemployment was accompanied by increased inequality.)

And third, the "Thatcher effect"—if it was that—began to dissipate after a few years, but the UK then received another shot in the arm, when, as noted earlier, the sterling devaluation of September 1992 brought about a major reduction of unemployment as compared in particular to France.[11] Too much should not be read out of a simple comparison of time series, but both of the British gains are based in part on a well-known fact of European political economy: Since joining the Community in 1972, the United Kingdom has maintained a degree of independence that has been either unwanted or unachievable by the other members. Even before Thatcher, the UK rejected continental *dirigisme*. Thatcher and Thatcherism emphasized that rejection and other differences. Had she remained in office, the British arm's length from Europe would have become the length of a football field.

She did not remain in office, however, which demonstrates the limit of anti-European tendencies in British politics. Her increasing rejection of EU was one of the chief reasons why she was forced out in 1992. The pro-European wing of the Conservative Party was no longer willing to tolerate her increasing Europe-bashing (or thought that the electorate was no longer willing to tolerate it, which in politics comes to the same thing), and they had a majority within the Tory membership of the House of Commons.

---

[11]The German figures after 1989 lose definition. Even though the continuing series is for West Germany, the economic basis for the data and to some extent the data themselves are strongly affected by the sudden unification with the East.

The subsequent history of British politics indicates the limits beyond which the Conservative Party cannot go in the other—pro-European—direction, but not quite the limits beyond which Britain cannot go. John Major, the new prime minister, was no integration extremist; British withdrawal from the exchange-rate mechanism of the EMS took place early in his term in that position. Nonetheless, as a middle-of-the-party choice for leadership, he was moderately European, as a result of which he has been vilified, particularly in recent years, by the vocal, strongly anti-Europe, Tory minority. It is in fact a minority: Major not only beat them hands down in the July 1995 showdown he forced, but the most likely successor had he lost would have been Michael Heseltine, even more strongly European than he was. Nonetheless, the Tory anti-Europeans currently prevent Major, if he were inclined that way, from moving any closer to integration on any important economic or political issue without risking losing to a coalition within his party that is tired enough of him personally and afraid enough of his negative political weight to risk substituting someone else. Major's precariousness has been highlighted more recently from the other side, by the defection to the centrist Liberal Democrats of a Tory MP for whom the government was too *anti*-European.

Major's popularity is in fact extremely low, and if one believes the polls and all of the other straws in the wind, the Tories are quite unlikely to win the next general election, due by 1997. A Labour win, however, will not mark a revolution—far from it. Under its new leader, Tony Blair, the party has recognized that, to win an election in the United Kingdom, it must become centrist—left-centrist to be sure, but that just means carrying out better and more fairly the things that Thatcher started. Britain in mid-decade is not riven by the society-dividing issue of immigration affecting France and other parts of the continent. Race, class, and youth problems exemplified by disturbances in some northern cities in the summer of 1995 do exist, but at least so long as the overall unemployment rate remains relatively low, they seem to be in hand. As in the United States, they may affect the tone of politics but they will not revolutionize it. The last British event anything like the French (and other continental) disturbances of 1968 was the General Strike of 1926. Now the British tend more to take out their hostilities in discussions of the various members of the royal family.

Major changes in foreign policy seem even less likely than in the domestic arena. In a tidal shift that has taken place over a period of decades, the Labour opposition has become more pro-European than the Conservatives. (The potentially balance-of-power Liberal Democrats are the most European of all.) This might be taken to presage a British move toward Europe if the Tories lost the next election, but it is in fact likely to be a small move at best. Labour has an anti-Europe wing, but it is smaller and certainly less vocal than that of the Conservatives, although the quiescence may be due mainly to Labourites' overwhelming desire to remain united long enough to win an election for a change. In any case, the "poetry"[12] of a Labour or a Lib-Lab coalition government may be better attuned to EU than the Major government. At least, the anti-Europe Tories would become a minority of a minority.

Real change, however, is likely to be less; Labour's positions are not very distant from those of Major's middle Conservatives. The United Kingdom, while the least likely among the major members of EU to want to surrender any degree of sovereignty to EU, is also the least likely to make additional waves. The British position is what it is, and as the exit of the pound from EMS demonstrated, it will remain what the British want it to be without deference to the other members, certainly not to the European Commission, EU's central bureaucratic governing body. And the British position is closer to that of de Gaulle than are most of the French Gaullists—a *Europe des patries* on the economic, as well as the political, side.

Economically, the British are opposed to the single currency. Assuming that the UK has rejoined the European currency system by the time when the real decisions on EMU must be finally made, the British under any government are likely to hold out for a loose model retaining a residual capability to act independently. And viewed from 1996, that seems the most probable outcome for the "single currency" at least by the year 2005.

Politically, the UK will remain very reluctant to surrender any further decisionmaking power to any supranational body, particularly but not only the European Commission. The one likely change under a

---

[12]See p. 2.

Labour government would be the adherence to the EU's "social charter" dictating various working and bargaining conditions. The
Conservatives have been quite unwilling to join in that. Labour will,
but the charter is primarily a statement of principles not very en-
forceable under EU's current governance, and no British government
is likely to want to tighten that governance very much.

Indeed, a major British concern with EU's recent expansion has been
to ensure that the expansion would not dilute the UK's power to exert an effective veto on issues that require less-than-unanimous
agreement under the EU charter. This also guides the British view of
further expansion to the states of central Europe. In principle, the
UK is mildly in favor of such expansion, but wants to redefine the
"qualified majority" that can win a vote in the Council of Ministers to
make it unlikely that any coalition can override the UK and the few
staunch allies it might be able to marshal. A Labour government
might have a more relaxed attitude on some of these issues, but not a
reversed position.

Neither is Labour likely to change substantially Britain's position on
NATO and the relationship with the United States. To the extent that
the "special relationship" implies special deference by one side to
the other simply because of kinship, it has attenuated. That thread
has been so slender for so many years, however, that further thinning
makes little difference. What remains and is more important is the
high-tensile-strength inner wire of real interests. It is instructive, for
example, that in all the controversy about the French need to engage
in some final nuclear tests to assure and calibrate their weapons, no
hint ever arose that Britain might want to resume testing. That was
both because the British are so well connected into the American
database and modeling system that they have no more need than the
United States for further testing and because they are so dependent
on the United States that they could not operate independently if
they wanted to. In any case, nuclear testing provides just one example of the continuing relationship at various military levels, most
likely to persist whatever happens to transatlantic politics.

Even politically, so long as the British need reinforcement against the
gravitational attraction of the continent and so long as the United
States can use this British need to retain a European ear predisposed
to listen, some "specialness" will remain. On what has been a prin-

cipal divisive issue, the relationship of specifically European military forces to the Atlantic Alliance as a whole, the UK has moved toward the French view of separability within NATO, but this has been within a general context of much less American hostility toward such a move by the Clinton administration as compared to the Bush administration.

The bottom line, however, for the United Kingdom, as with Germany and France, is that internal developments are likely to govern external policies. And among the big three, Britain's inner workings are most likely to remain the most stable.

Chapter Three

THE EUROPEAN UNION

The future course of the European Union will depend on three closely related sets of decisions:

- The speed and shape of further economic integration, revolving around the single currency

- The possibility and shape of increasingly integrated political decisionmaking, particularly on security and other matters of foreign policy

- The speed and conditions of admission of new members, mainly from central Europe.

Each of these issues will be determined primarily by the interplay among the Big Three and other current members of EU. The economics of the rest of the world, particularly the United States and Japan, will also have important effects on economic and political integration, however.

ECONOMIC INTEGRATION

The 1991 Maastricht Treaty scheduled the third and final stage of the European Monetary Union (EMU)—the introduction of a single currency, a European central bank, and a consequent common monetary policy—for 1997 at the earliest and 1999 at the latest. The 1997 date has long been seen as unrealistic, and it was officially abandoned in the summer of 1995. The question now is whether even the 1999 deadline can be met.[1]

The concept has been that, as of the target date, EU member states that have fulfilled a strict set of economic-fiscal-monetary "convergence" criteria will become members of EMU. This will be automatic for all members except the United Kingdom and Denmark, which have reserved the right to opt out. Unless all EU members become members of EMU, EU will then proceed at "two speeds," for those members in EMU and those remaining outside.

Given the relative economic weights of EU's member nations, the central questions for establishment of a single-currency-based EMU are: Will Britain, Germany, and France meet the convergence criteria? And will they then join? The second question has some relevance not only to Britain, which has reserved its options, but even to Germany and France, which ostensibly have not, because grumbling in both countries about whether a single currency is really needed has in fact been increasing lately. In any case, Germany plus one of the other two seems necessary: An EMU without Germany is unthinkable; a single currency without either France or the UK added to Germany would be little more than a minor extension of the deutsche mark.

The convergence criteria are:

- *Price Stability.* An inflation rate no more than 1.5 percentage points higher than the average of the lowest three member states.

- *Exchange Rate Stability.* Remaining within the normal fluctuating margins for exchange rates under the current EMS for two years. De facto, "normal" is being defined around 2 percent. This is much less than the 15 percent allowed by EMS.

---

[1]The factual but not the predictive and analytical portions of this discussion of the single currency crib liberally from Christine Detournet, *Economic and Monetary Union: Toward a Single Currency,* a mimeographed report produced in Brussels in February 1995. The report bears no further identification, but it was probably prepared for the European Commission.

- *Long-Term Interest Rates.* Long-term rates no more than 2 percentage points higher than the three states with the lowest rates of inflation.

- *Budgetary Discipline.* A government deficit no more than 3 percent of GDP and a total government debt no more than 60 percent of GDP. This criterion effectively precludes the use of fiscal stimulus to encourage economic growth or even to combat recession.

The European Commission expects that, by 1996, Germany and France will meet the first three criteria. Britain is within bounds on the third, interest rates, but having temporarily dropped out of the existing European Payment System, remains outside on exchange rates. With regard to inflation, the "Commission forecasts that in 1996 . . . the United Kingdom [is] expected to remain outside the desired bracket."[2] However, the British seem likely to be able come within bounds on both exchange and inflation rates by 1999 if they want to.

It is the last criterion, "Budgetary Discipline," specifically the requirement that the current deficit/GDP ratio not exceed 3 percent, that provides the toughest test. In 1995, even Germany failed the deficit-limit test, as did every EU member except Luxembourg—this although none of them even implicitly espoused deliberate fiscal stimulus. In fact, in spite of brave statements by both German and French officials, convergence by 1999 is increasingly unlikely.

Implementation at a later date of an EMU close to the current design will be a question of will and willingness for each of the Big Three.

The UK is not committed to the single currency; as noted, this is true for both the Labour opposition and the Tory government. Nonetheless, if a Labour government is in power when decision time comes, an EMU that included Germany and France might be difficult to resist; this would be even truer for a Labour–Liberal Democrat coalition.

---

[2]Detournet (1995), p. 4. The Commission's table, "Prévisions d'évolution des principaux critères de convergence de 1993–1995," which actually goes on to 1996, is appended to Detournet's paper and appears to show the UK within this criterion for 1995 and 1996.

For France, *le franc fort* represents a strong commitment to the single currency, but the next legislative elections come before the final decision on EMU. Going into the elections, the commitment to *le franc fort* may weaken, particularly if public opinion polls show the government majority ebbing because of continued high unemployment. Consequent effective devaluation of the franc within the 15-percent limits would not violate the guidelines of the current EMS, but it would carry France outside the bounds of "normal" exchange rate fluctuation called for by the new EMU, and thus force postponement of the single currency. Indeed, if unemployment remains high, the overall French commitment to political and economic integration may be further weakened by the results of the legislative elections.

Meanwhile, however, Germany has been moving in the opposite direction—toward imposing even tougher requirements for any European currency that might dare to replace the deutsche mark. This too could change, however, if German unemployment continues to increase, thus forcing a choice between attending to internal problems and returning to convergence. Indeed, as noted above, Germany may be on the way to economic and consequent social problems similar to those of the French. If such problems become acute, all bets are off.

An explicit retreat from EMU is thus a possibility. More probable, however, would be a less clear-cut outcome. Economic pressures in France and similar pressures within Germany could well lead to mutual French-German agreement to weaken the proposed structure of EMU or to postpone the date. One possibility that has been discussed would be a new European currency coexisting with the old ones and a new central bank also coexisting, rather than a single currency and central bank. This would be disappointing for many officials and the citizens in both countries, but the German-French agreement on the issue would preserve one essential—the continued political closeness of the two states. Postponement for several years beyond 1999 would also be possible. The question then, however, would be whether Europe can tread water or whether postponement would inevitably lead to a major retreat from integration.

The game will not be played entirely within EU. The other major centers of economic power, the United States and Japan (perhaps over the time period considered here, this will become East Asia more generally), may also play important roles, in two ways. One, the effect on EU of external competition, will most probably have little impact on the EMU timetable; the other, the effects of non-European economic centers on the world business cycle, is potentially major.

Changes in the structure of world trade take a long time, and with the conclusion of the Uruguay Round and the conversion of the General Agreement on Tariffs and Trade (GATT) into the World Trade Organization (WTO), the new institutions are likely to shake down and stabilize over the next ten years. A new round of negotiations may begin within that period, but such negotiations themselves stretch out over many years.

The chief effects on EMU integration of competition from its west and east will therefore be within the current framework. Trade pressures will almost certainly increase, particularly as new industrial nations come on line. These will weigh at least initially on traditional lines of endeavor, of which automobiles remain the prototype. Since the possibilities for EU protection as a conscientious participant in WTO are limited, the effects may be felt in pushing EU further in the high-tech directions in which it would like to move anyhow, but the high-tech competition from the United States and Asia will remain fierce. Whether EU will be able to exploit the opening markets in Asia, which one way or another are likely to remain de facto protectionist, is questionable. If markets begin to open more rapidly in central Europe and the former Soviet Union, however, West Europe, particularly Germany, will be better situated.

All in all, however, the effect of world competition seems most likely to put a little more pressure on the EU members attempting to grow out of their high rates of unemployment, which may in turn make it a little harder to move toward economic integration. On the other hand, stiff competition may also induce more of a fortress mentality within EU as a whole. That would affect EU's relationship with the rest of the world and perhaps push toward internal integration. In any case, trade pressures are not likely to force major changes in the timetable or structure of EMU.

The effects of world macroeconomic events are potentially more traumatic. Nobody has abolished the business cycle, but in recent decades it has been manageable, and European monetary and fiscal authorities seem well able to manage it. As has been pointed out here, the *primus inter* these *pares*, the Bundesbank, has a conservative bias toward fighting inflation at the cost of reduced growth. However, the elders who run the bank may yet be wise enough to marshal their resources against the threat of a real downturn.

Such a degree of wisdom may be less likely for Japan and the United States. In early 1996, Japan was still in the grips of a major recession that had already continued for several years, concealing its severity by continuing to run low ostensible unemployment rates because of the lingering effects of Japanese "lifetime employment." With the political system frozen and the bureaucracy fossilized, it is not clear that what has to be done in the way of expansionary fiscal and monetary policy will be done. With some issues of debt and related structures unresolved, the potential remains for a crash, in either the short or the long run. Such a crash would have an immense international impact.

The current situation in the United States is far better. If fiscal policy is fixed in concrete, however, by either a balanced budget amendment or a political equivalent that makes virtually impossible any deficit response to a downturn—already made glacierlike by constitutional checks and balances—the potential for catastrophe will be significant.

Economic disaster in Japan or the United States would quickly spread to EU. Ideally, that might cause the members to work together to protect themselves, but such ideals are seldom reached. A pulling back into nationalistic shells would be more expectable.

Withal, such a disaster is possible but not probable. It still seems reasonable to set the *canonical* prediction for EMU and the single currency at the following: Some slippage in the 1999 deadline and perhaps also the Maastricht criteria, without a major retreat on either.

POLITICAL INTEGRATION

The canonical slow but steady pace toward economic integration provides a relatively positive and also realistic standpoint from which to examine the issues of political integration, those relating to security and other aspects of foreign policy in particular.

It is relatively positive because, if instead we were to begin by looking at political integration in relative isolation from economic integration and EMU, matters would appear to be still moving very slowly as of 1996. In the realm of security, recent events demonstrate that

- British and French inhibitions to operational military cooperation are slowly eroding; the forces of the two worked together on an ad hoc basis in Yugoslavia with little apparent friction. Germany, however, is willing to play only to a very limited extent. Proposals are being made in unofficial circles for joint Anglo-French nuclear planning as a first step toward more general integration,[3] and President Chirac has made symbolic noises in that direction, but they are very far from operational implementation.

- Joint procurement is a mixed bag. On the one hand, British purchase of the Apache soured British-French cooperation, at least temporarily. On the other hand, several French satellite developments are being shared or are likely to be shared in the future with other European allies.

- The Eurocorps provides a structure within which Germany and France can plan and train with each other and with other continental members of EU, but whether the corps will ever find a situation in which it can be politically and militarily operable is a very open question.

- The Western European Union (WEU), EU's military arm, is a symbol for the future and a potential matrix for future integrated planning, but currently not much more. France's rapproche-

---

[3]See, for example, Olivier Debouzy, "A European Vocation for the French Nuclear Deterrent," in Nicholas Witney, Olivier Debouzy, and Robert Levine, *West European Nuclear Forces: A British, a French and an American View*, Santa Monica, Calif.: RAND, MR-587-AF, 1995.

ment with the NATO military structure moves it closer to other states that belong both to NATO and WEU.

- And anyhow, the total military force available to the European Union falls short on such functions as intelligence, transport, and some aspects of close air support and of logistics, all of which have had to be supplied by the United States. The likelihood that the member states will increase military expenditures for EU to remedy these deficiencies using their own resources is close to zero.

This does not suggest promising prospects for joint EU military capabilities.

Military issues, however, are at least relatively concrete compared to those of integrated decisionmaking in more general foreign policy and other areas, let alone constitutional theorizing. Thought and discourse here tend to start with the abstract: Should EU move toward becoming a "federation" as is advocated more or less explicitly by many Germans; or should it stay as it is and as the British would like it to remain—a customs union with enough additional policies to accommodate an inevitably integrating economy?

Some of the abstract arguments do come down to concrete questions concerning such matters as the size of less-than-unanimous "qualified majorities" of the members to decide on various specified matters, or the decision powers of the European Commission and of the European Parliament in other areas. Actions needed to keep the integrated economy running—allowable public subsidies to private firms, competition, agriculture—are very real issues and require decisions in which national governments are sometimes overridden by qualified majorities. Nonetheless, for security and other aspects of foreign policy, it is quite clear that Bonn, Paris, and London retain full control over their own forces and policies, and they are not to be overridden by Brussels or Strasbourg. Neither is there any evidence that this is changing or will change in the foreseeable future, toward the abstraction of a "common foreign policy." Commonality in these areas is interesting to debate, particularly for French Cartesians and other EU intellectuals, but the debates show no signs of producing compelling concepts that promise to change future structures.

What may be significantly more realistic, however, are political integration and ultimately security and foreign policy integration proceeding from the real rather than the abstract, from increasing economic integration rather than philosophical contention. *The crucial step here will be the first one. Once the members states enter into an EMU operating with a single currency, the steps leading to a federal Europe are likely to follow one another down a preordained primrose path.*

The canonical economic prediction is mildly positive about the likelihood of integration: If nothing much goes wrong, EMU and a single currency are coming—neither as fast nor as clear-cut as some would prefer, but they are coming. Such a common monetary policy would be a very powerful tool governing the most basic national interests of employment and every other aspect of prosperity in each of the member states. Indeed, as has been contended above, France's central current problem is that French prosperity is being managed for Paris by Frankfurt.

Even if the new European bank is also in Frankfurt, however, it will have to base its actions on economic conditions west of the Rhine and south of the Alps, as well as those within Germany. France and the other non-German members will thus gain from EMU at least a small degree of control over Western Europe's economy, control that they do not now have over the Bundesbank, which in reality now rules; indeed, that is the problem for many Germans. Control of the new central bank will not be by governments—the European Bank will be "independent" of politics, as the Bundesbank and the Banque de France are now, but at least non-German nationals will help make the decisions. What the new members of EMU will lose in exchange for this degree of control, however, will be revocability. Under the current looser system, they can break away as the UK (and Italy) have; once a single currency is in place, for one of the Big Three to return again to a national currency might well destroy EU in its entirety, a risk unlikely to be taken.

By losing control over their monetary policies, the members of EMU will lose a large measure of control over their fiscal policies as well. The common, if simplified, view of national fiscal policies is that sovereign governments can finance desired expenditures either by taxing or by "printing money." In recent years, the printing has been figurative in the wealthy nations, which can create money by borrowing from their own central banks, but historically and in some of the more desperate current states, e.g., parts of the former Soviet Union, the presses have in fact turned out a lot of unbacked currency.

Carried to an excess, either printing or borrowing to finance economic growth can lead to major economic problems culminating in hyperinflation, but carefully done under various circumstances, they can be quite workable and acceptable. This will become impossible for individual states, however, once they lose control over their own money to EMU. Literal printing would definitionally be outlawed under a true single currency; de facto printing-by-borrowing would become almost equally impossible, because neither the European Bank or anyone else would provide more than emergency loans under those circumstances.

That, not greater morality, is why the states of the United States balance their budgets, whereas the federal government has not done so since 1969: The federal government can print money. To be sure, some states try to deceive themselves and others for short periods of time about what a balanced budget is, but they generally suffer for it. With a few supportable exceptions (e.g., bond financing of capital improvements), the states, unlike the federal government, can increase spending only at the cost of increasing taxes. And the same constraint prevents individual states from insulating themselves to pursue their own growth-stimulating fiscal policies. That is also possible only for the federal government.

A single-currency EMU will put its members into the same position as the states of the United States. To some extent, in fact, they are already there; the Bundesbank governs. As Britain has shown, it is still possible to get out from under that governance, but under EMU, it will no longer be so.

But if fiscal policy can no longer be determined by the individual nations, who will direct it? Two answers are possible:

- The first is that nobody will direct. Fiscal policy will be governed by rule, probably a balanced budget rule with little or no discretion allowed. To conservative economists, this seems highly desirable; it is currently seen as desirable in theory by many politicians, particularly in the United States. It was also seen as desirable in the 1920s. When the Crash and the Great Depression arrived, however, the fixed fiscal rule suddenly became very undesirable. In fact, the political desirability of a single rule is mainly theoretical even now. It would take much less than the Great Depression, in the United Sates and Europe, to call for strong demands for an active fiscal policy, although in the United States, constitutional or political gridlock might preclude rapid response to those demands.

- The other answer on fiscal governance is that, either in anticipation of the need for an active fiscal policy or in response to the need, somebody in the EU will have to exert fiscal authority. But fiscal-budgetary authority is inherently political; a European fiscal institution will necessarily be a strong political and governmental institution. Once the fact and locus of such authority become clear, the individual member states will then still be able to control their budgets with the limited degree of flexibility that the American states have. In the fiscal realm, however, they will no longer be sovereign; some set of EU decisionmakers will.

The rest seems likely to follow. Once the decisionmakers of the European Union gain fiscal power, security and foreign policy power will appear much less out of reach than they now seem. The United States of Europe will not mimic the United States of America—certainly not in name—but it could be remarkably similar. The "democratic deficit" inherent in decisionmaking by European Commission bureaucrats might even drive the European Parliament in Strasbourg toward becoming a real legislature.

None of this is a prediction, canonical or otherwise. If it does happen, it is likely to take more than the next ten or so millennium-crossing years. And if it does happen, it may not include all EU members; the UK in particular, sensing a scenario like that described, might opt out at an early stage. In any case, there is no certainty that it will happen at all.

What is contended here, however, is that, if a federal Europe does come, it is far more likely to happen this way than through suspicious military cooperation and abstract foreign policy or other constitutional theorizing.

EU EXPANSION

The third necessary set of decisions is that concerning the admission of new members: mainly the former Communist states of central Europe—the Czech Republic, Slovakia, Poland, Hungary, Bulgaria, Romania, and Slovenia; perhaps eventually the Baltic states of Estonia, Latvia, and Lithuania; someday maybe even Ukraine. The Mediterranean island states of Malta and Cyprus are also knocking on the door. Turkey has been knocking for a long time, but that door seems destined to remain shut.

EU expansion raises difficult political and economic issues made more difficult by the constitutional and bureaucratic processes for admission of new members. Admission procedures are long and cumbersome and require unanimity on the part of the existing members. There seems no way that the new applicants could move through the machinery until sometime after 2000, and that could take place only with a strong consensus on the part of the current membership. With consensus, unanimity might become possible— small members can be browbeaten—but for political and economic reasons, no consensus exists in any case.

Politically, it is feared that significant numbers of new members would change the nature of the organization under its current rules. That fear was present even for the most recent admissions, of Austria, Finland, and Sweden, states that are politically and economically very similar to the existing members. If EU in the future were to become a true federation, then the problem might be no greater than the admission of new states to the United States: Accept our constitution and join us; you get two seats in the Senate and an appropriate number in the House of Representatives; and majorities and "qualified majorities," like two-thirds for overriding vetoes, are constitutionally set and are adjusted mathematically for new admissions.

Under EU's current structure, however, admission procedures are less automatic and politically more difficult. As has been noted, the British fear the weakening of the qualified majorities that existed when the EU had twelve members. The UK could then block an antithetical measure requiring a three-quarters majority by recruiting— say—Portugal, Spain, and Denmark. Adaptations have been made for the recent expansion of EU membership from 12 to 15, but this would become more difficult with the accession of more new members. Suppose, for example, that the newly entered Czech Republic, Poland, Hungary, and Slovenia were all to join a continental entente that could thus override the UK?

Matters like the requirements for qualified majorities for various decisions are adjustable, but not automatically or even simply. Adjustment is highly political and will inevitably delay decisions on admission. The same is true for issues relating to the necessary democratic governance of prospective members. Some, like the Czech Republic, seem irreversibly democratic; some are stabilizing their democracies; others still remain in doubt. For the latter cases in particular, examination, adjudication, and negotiation will take time; again, the process will be a slow one.

Consistent with the theme of this analysis, however, the highest obstacles are likely to be the economic ones. EU is not a symbolic organization or one oriented primarily to meeting contingent future needs. It is a very real operating institution, with immense implications for the current as well as the future economic interests of its members. New members will have to

- have economies based firmly on free market principles and practices

- be close enough to existing members in GDP per capita as not to increase significantly the subsidies paid by wealthy members to poorer ones, decrease the subsidies now received by the poorer ones by forcing the sharing out of limited pots, or cause significant migrant flows over newly opened borders

- not hurt significant interest groups in the existing member states by the competition of goods flowing freely over the newly opened borders.

The ease with which Austria, Finland, and Sweden fulfilled all of the entrance qualifications highlights by contrast the difficulties the criteria will present for the next tranche.

The simplest of these issues is the free market, like democracy a sine qua non for entry. Most of the potential applicants have been moving toward free markets in their own interests, which coincide with the ideology of EU.

The need for subsidies and the possible effects of new admissions on flows of people and of goods, however, are very real and potentially very costly to existing members. Three poor states, each with histories similar to those of the current applicants, have been admitted to EU (then EEC, the European Economic Community) since its inception. Portugal and Spain had recently overthrown long-term fascist regimes, Greece a shorter-lived military dictatorship. As with the current applicants from the former Communist world, the West European nations of EEC wanted to cement these prodigal children into democracy, but unlike the central European states, each was a small and individual case with costs that did not appear to loom large at the time of admission.

The new applicants are coming in waves. The first is the so-called "Visegrad" group, countries that threw the communist regimes over, threw them out, and began moving immediately toward democracy and more slowly toward free markets. To be sure, of the original three, only the Czech half of the former Czechoslovakia remains firmly on the original course. The other two and a half—Poland, Hungary, and the Slovak part of Czechoslovakia—have since returned former communists to some degree of power, but these parties and individuals seem truly reformed, if for no other reason than that they have decided that capitalist power and wealth is what they are after, not a return to communism. The past is not the issue for the Visegrad states (or for Slovenia, which has many similarities). Rather, the problem is the fact that they are still poor and, relative to the nations of Western Europe, will remain so for quite some time. Admission, even in the early 2000s, would be costly to EU in terms of subsidies, competition, and potential migration. So would the admission of the other applicants and likely future applicants, Malta and Cyprus, as well as Bulgaria, Romania, and the Baltic states.

Looking outward from 1996, it seems improbable that the members of EU will be ready to bear the costs of the new admissions willingly, at least not until the costs have been reduced by further economic growth. Indeed, admission would appear close to impossible if the nations of Western Europe are still struggling with their own high unemployment rates and constraining budget deficits. Germany, in particular, which will inevitably be the chief bearer of costs for the new members, will still be underwriting the reconstruction of its own east; France is likely to be looking south to similar problems of instability in the Maghreb and consequent migration pressures.

The central motivation for the nations of Western Europe to draw their eastern neighbors into the fold will remain: stabilization of democracy and security on their eastern borders. Achieving this by bringing the central European states into EU, however, will be a long and difficult process. Rather, NATO looks like an easier and cheaper route, and besides, bringing them in through NATO would also involve the United States in the task.

Chapter Four

NATO

Involving the United States in Europe was always a central purpose of NATO; with the end of the Cold War, it has become the only one of the original purposes remaining in more than a vestigial form. It is still a purpose of high importance to both the United States and Europe, which is why concern exists about what some see as a dangerous crumbling of the Alliance.

This chapter begins with a discussion of the narrowing down of NATO functions from the Cold War to the present, then takes up three issues for the future of the Alliance:

- The potential for crumbling

- An additional new function: stabilizing the nations of central Europe by bringing them in

- Possible new military missions.

THE NARROWING OF FUNCTIONS

The Cold-War wisecrack-become-cliché about NATO was that the functions of the Alliance were "To keep the Russians out, the Americans in, and the Germans down."

The first of these, keeping the Russians out, has become *almost* obsolete. True, the logic suggesting that the Russian military forces, which are having great difficulties in defeating Chechnya, can present no threat to the West is a bit too facile. The military tasks are very different, as they were in the parallel situation when American military might, even while losing in Vietnam, remained quite sufficient to deter Soviet aggression against the United States and Western Europe. Nonetheless, all the evidence surrounding current Russian forces is that they are weak and in a state of disarray. That they could fight their way through Ukraine and Poland to threaten Germany or the rest of Western Europe is obviously ludicrous. Even more important than the current balance, however, is the very long time it would take for Russia's economy and society to rebuild to the point where they could again support forces that might present a danger to the West. By that time, Russia, the West, and the rest of the world will be so changed that such a future danger should have little bearing on current decisions about NATO.

The one real residuum from the past that makes Russia "almost" a non-threat rather than absolutely a non-threat is its continued possession of a powerful nuclear arsenal. But NATO as such has little to do with deterring any potential Russian nuclear threats. Rather, as has always been the case, the task falls to the United States, aided by the British and perhaps the French nuclear forces (or maybe in the future a European force based on those two).

"Keeping the Russians out" has thus disappeared from NATO's mission. "Keeping the Germans down" was already obsolete long before the end of the Cold War. Germany's decades-old role as the keystone of Western Europe certainly presents problems for the other nations, but these are the economic and political problems working their way through EU and EMU. German security will remain integrated into European (and Atlantic) security so long as German economics and politics remain integrated into European economics and politics.

NATO is still relevant, but it is relevant because of the third of its original roles—providing the institutional basis for "keeping the Americans in." Keeping the Americans in Europe remains a vital interest on both sides of the Atlantic:

- For the Western Europeans,
  - A continued American presence through NATO remains crucial because in Europe as it is, as compared to Europe as it ought to be and perhaps some day will be, the United States continues to provide the only organizational direction capable of pulling mutual interests together into cooperative ac-

tions. This was proven again in the summer and fall of 1995, when the United States brought its allies together into complementary military and diplomatic activities that offered the first real hopes of ending the slaughter in Bosnia. To be sure, this seeming success followed years of failure; it worked only when the time was right and the mutual interests of the NATO allies were aligned.   Whether this constitutes American "leadership" is a moot and emotional point not worth the semantic controversy it generates. Certainly, French President Chirac provided at least a partial initial catalyst, but France could not pull together the military alliance to which it did not even formally belong. The United States could and did.

— Additionally, the U.S. presence continues to be important to many Europeans as a political counterweight to Germany, still deeply desired by France and other nations and even by Germany itself, which feels uncomfortable with its history and with its neighbors' fears of German history.

• For the United States, West European stability remains a vital interest

— Europe continues to be America's essential economic partner. NATO may not seem the clear choice as a vehicle for expressing U.S. economic interests, but it provides much the strongest existing transatlantic link as EU continues on its stately pace toward self-directed integration. So long as Europeans continue to desire American security participation for the reasons just discussed, this provides Americans with significant bargaining power even in the economic sphere.

— In purer security terms, the question is no longer that of "losing" Western Europe as it was during World War II and the Cold War. Should Europe become internally unstable, however, either within individual nations, as has been suggested is possible for France, or because of centrifugal forces within EU, the United States might begin to be concerned with its own security in a nuclear world. The history of having to rescue Europe twice in a century may be more relevant existentially than historically, but it has not been forgotten.

All this is why the possibility that NATO might crumble causes concern on both sides of the Atlantic.

IS NATO CRUMBLING?

The answer to the question depends on the aspect of NATO under examination.

Since the breakup first of the Warsaw Pact and then of the Soviet Union, no one has doubted that NATO would have to change radically, with the change including substantial downsizing of forces. That has happened: The vital and active Alliance of the Cold War is a shadow of what it once was, inevitably so. Equally inevitably, the change has led to a feeling of malaise among individuals and institutions that had participated in NATO in its full glory. Nonetheless, the organization in which 16 nations plan together, politically and militarily, and in 1995 acted together, has by no means disappeared, and any danger of its doing so is far from imminent.

Within the range running from Cold War vigor down to actual disappearance, "crumbling" may be defined operationally to mean, not disappearance (which the laws of bureaucracy suggest is unlikely in any case), but rather loss of NATO's capability to fulfill its essential function. The question for the future is whether NATO will become an insufficient vehicle for maintaining that function—American participation in West European affairs. And the summary answer is: Not necessarily, but if enough things are done badly enough, perhaps the crumbling of NATO could happen.

Any fears, however, should be for the future, not the present. On a simple, current steady-state basis, the answer on whether NATO is crumbling is "no." The post–Cold-War structural adjustments have been made; U.S. troop levels have been drawn down to less than a third of their peak numbers; political NATO, headed by a European Secretary-General, remains in a large building in Brussels; military NATO, headed by an American Supreme Commander, remains in a complex of buildings in Mons, Belgium. Regular meetings and planning continue. In fact, two favorable developments have taken place: "Partnership for Peace" has established at least an interim relationship between NATO and not only central European states but also Russia, and the French have relaxed the rigor with which they explicitly eschewed participation in the NATO military structure. When the Alliance, including the French, finally got its act together politically, it was still able to produce a strong military effort in Bosnia.

Nonetheless, the question has been asked not only, "Is NATO now crumbling?" but "Is NATO now in crisis?" Paradoxically, the answer to the second may well be "yes," even though the answer to the first remains "no." NATO was in apparent crisis, at least through the late summer of 1995, because of its signal failure up until then to achieve any significant degree of either pacification or justice in the former Yugoslavia. The failure was caused in part by divisions among NATO's members over alternative courses of action; it in turn exacerbated those divisions, particularly between France and the United Kingdom on the one side and the United States on the other. NATO's move into Bosnia in 1995 and 1996 solved the immediate crisis in the Alliance; whether it will lead to a longer-run internal détente remains to be seen.

What should have been done or should be done in Yugoslavia lies outside the scope of this discussion. The lack of agreement among NATO's leading members did in fact cause a crisis within the organization, but crises within NATO are hardly new. One can count: France's withdrawal from the military organization in 1966; the early-1980s decision by European members, strongly objected to by the United States, to finance a Soviet natural gas pipeline at the height of the Cold War; disagreements in the 1980s over conventional disarmament; major clashes in the early 1980s over the installation of intermediate-range nuclear missiles in Europe and in the late 1980s over their withdrawal by treaty with the Soviet Union; and throughout, the chronic quarrel with recurring critical spells over American concepts of nuclear deterrence (fight a convincing conventional battle against a Soviet attack before going nuclear if the battle is lost) versus European (face an immediate choice between escalating and losing).

These Cold War crises, sharp as some of them were, never put the existence and functioning of NATO into question. In spite of occasional threats, even by some responsible Americans (e.g., Senator Sam Nunn), of reduced U.S. participation, there was virtually no chance of the United States either pulling out or being pushed. The reason, of course, was what was perceived as the continuing threat of the Soviet Union to Western Europe and to U.S. interests in Western Europe.

That counterweight has now disappeared, which has led to fears that crises like Bosnia may cause future crumbling. If NATO could not over a period of years agree on common action in a situation like Yugoslavia, when and how can it function in the future? In particular, if the United States, as the nominal "leader" of the Alliance, was unable to lead during those years, what is the meaning of that leadership? True, in 1995 and 1996, American leadership and Alliance cohesion were restored, even more strongly, by NATO's first actual military operation. If, as seems likely however, U.S. troops are withdrawn on the current schedule in November 1996 without any solid solution of Yugoslavia's problems, tensions within NATO may again increase.

As mentioned above, the major lesson from Yugoslavia is that, for now and at least the short-run future, it is clear that NATO can function only with consensus among its leading members that their vital interests are at stake.[1] That was the case in the Persian Gulf, but in Yugoslavia, in contrast, it was not clear for a long time whose interests were engaged how. Germany helped start the crisis by its pressure for rapid recognition of Croatia, but then did not participate; France and Britain blundered in with lightly armed "peacekeeping" troops, encouraged initially by the United States, which kept its own ground forces out. Only with the dual catalysts of Croat routing of the Serbs in Krajina followed by a brutal Bosnian Serb attempt to sabotage possibilities of a negotiated peace did the major NATO participants begin to come together.

Even so, the years of disagreement did not lead to any concurrent crumbling—no threats from the United States or European members to abandon the Alliance or reduce contributions, for example. If anything, the crisis without a crumble demonstrated the strength rather than the weakness of the Alliance. The events, however, did throw into question American "leadership." That history might be discussed in great detail, but it can be summarized by saying that, under

---

[1]Under current French usage, if an *interêt* is *vital*, it will be covered by *dissuasion nucléaire* (nuclear deterrence). The term "vital interests" is used more broadly here.

both the Bush and the Clinton administrations, the United States sporadically attempted to exert leadership of the Western effort in Yugoslavia (partly within NATO, partly within the UN) and sometimes retreated from leadership. Some of the times when the United States tried to lead, the Europeans rejected the leadership, e.g., when Secretary of State Christopher toured European capitals in 1993 on behalf of an active pro-Bosnian government policy. Only when the time was ripe in mid-1995 was U.S. leadership restored and, as noted, the time may soon become overripe without the improbable construction of a long-run solution for Yugoslavia.

As in the case of failure to function, blame for the failure of American leadership can be shared among the putative leader and the putative followers in any number of ways. What is more important is the demonstration that, just as consensus cannot be artificially constructed but must be consensus of national interests, leadership among the major members of NATO cannot be artificially imposed but must be based on consensus. This need not bring about a crumbling of NATO, so long as mutual recognition exists that the organization continues to fulfill the function, vital to both sides of the Atlantic, of keeping the Americans in.

Here is where the potential longer-run danger from the Yugoslav crisis lies, however—more on the American side than on the European, perhaps because the Europeans are more used to the practice of *realpolitik*. The long-time failure of the West to halt what was widely interpreted throughout the United States as the holocaust-like "ethnic cleansing" of Bosnian Muslims by Bosnian Serbs abetted by the Yugoslav government led some Americans to question whether NATO remains important and useful to the United States or whether American interests and beliefs might be better pursued unilaterally. The questioning is based in part on the continued Wilsonian component of American foreign policy—in this case, a disgust with the immorality of ethnic cleansing and with the perceived failure of NATO to act against that immorality. But this idealistic strain has long been present in American policy; by itself it has seldom overcome U.S. vital interests.

In part, also, the questioning of NATO is political. At least one candidate for the U.S. presidency, Pat Buchanan, is clearly isolationist; others have made an issue of international failures in Bosnia, and proposed going it alone regardless of the effect on U.S. allies with troops in harm's way. The saving grace of the more purely political line, however, may be that, if someone espousing it were to win the presidential election, the negative effect on U.S. participation in the Alliance might be less than it had seemed. A once-candidate, now-president could come to recognize that NATO remains the vehicle of choice for essential U.S. participation in Europe.

A longer-run potential danger to NATO, from within the United States and perhaps from Europe as well, is the difficulty in understanding and acknowledging something as insubstantial as "Keeping the Americans in" as the basis for a military alliance and for the real costs that it incurs. The 100,000 U.S. troops in Europe may be considered expensive at a time of severe budget-cutting, and if no concrete military mission for those troops can be made plausible, general "participation" in European affairs may not suffice. In 1991, I wrote that:

> it is difficult to sell a taxpaying electorate on the need to spend billions of dollars (or pounds or deutsche marks or francs) abroad for military power applied for other than military purposes—for the abstractions of "stability" or an American place at the European table. [Rather], a *military* rationale is needed, a "social myth."[2]

I suggested, as such a military rationale, hedging against a series of uncertainties, each of which was of low probability but which together multiplied out to a significant chance of *something* happening. I also expressed doubt that this could provide a politically sufficient basis for support of NATO into the indefinite future.

Five years later, I hope—and think—that my initial pessimism may have been misplaced. The political need for retaining NATO as a political-military vehicle for U.S. presence in Europe may be easier to admit to publicly than in the early post–Cold-War days when the Alliance was just phasing down from the glory of its 30-year role as a mighty military machine with a mighty military mission. The evidence shows that NATO has survived nicely both several years of disputes over Yugoslavia and severe budget pressures in all member

---

[2]Robert A. Levine, *European Security for the 1990s: Uncertain Prospects and Prudent Policies*, Santa Monica, Calif.: RAND, N-3240-RC, 1991, p. 31.

nations. Now, the continued need for a hedge against a series of military uncertainties, of which Yugoslavia and the Gulf War provide examples, together with the always-powerful force of bureaucratic and political inertia, may reinforce the real political function. Together they can form a strong rationale for continued participation in NATO by its current members, including the United States. Nonetheless, the search for alternative missions continues, and should.

NATO EXPANSION

One function that NATO has already added to "Keeping the Americans in" is "Keeping the Central Europeans stable." Expansion of NATO to the east—to Visegrad and the other Central European nations—is official NATO policy, and as President Clinton has said, it "is no longer a question of whether, but when and how."[3] That formulation, however, leaves the real issue wide open. The questions for this analysis are: Will the *when* of these nations joining NATO precede or succeed their joining EU, and will that *when* fall within the next five to ten years? And what are the conditions determining the *how?*

The debate over *when* expansion will occur is in some measure an extension of a debate over *whether*, which never really took place. NATO, led by the United States and Germany, was concerned enough by the entreaties of the Central European states and worried enough by their potential instability that the decision in principle to admit them was quickly arrived at. What was not recognized, however, until Russian Foreign Minister Andrei Kozyrev walked out of a 1994 NATO meeting in Brussels that had been intended to welcome Russia and Central Europe into "Partnership for Peace," was the strength of Russian opposition to NATO expansion toward its borders.

The strong Russian opposition in turn strengthened the hand of those in the West who had been dubious about the expansion. Since the decision to expand had already been made, however, the doubts have led instead to an ongoing and substantial discussion of *when*

---

[3]President Bill Clinton, Warsaw speech, July 1994.

and *how*. On the one side are those who still want to move rapidly, both because of fears for Central European stability and because they see expansion as a weapon against the crumbling of NATO.[4] On the other are those who are afraid that the destabilizing effects both on Russia's relations with the West and on its internal politics will outweigh the stabilizing effects in Central Europe, and who contend that, since the basic causes for potential instability in Central Europe are economic and political rather than a nonexistent military threat, the proper order of integration into the West would be EU first, then NATO.[5]

Those in a hurry want to proceed at full speed to NATO membership for Central European states without waiting for EU expansion to play out. One major reason is a growing understanding that the kinds of economic difficulties discussed above will inevitably slow down the pace of their entry into EU. NATO may thus provide a quicker and easier means of tying them into Western Europe and stability, a task that the proponents consider urgent.

The pressures for speed raise President Clinton's companion question to *when*: *how* the new applicants might be admitted into NATO—what conditions for expansion might in fact make it easy and rapid. It was suggested above that the major reason for slow progress toward expanding EU is that expansion will involve real economic costs that will not be easily accepted and will threaten real economic interests that would not be easily compromised. Yet, threats to security interests can be far more frightening than threats to economic interests, and costs to protect against the threats can be greater. Why then can NATO admission be made into an easier path than EU for the Central European states to enter the West?

The underlying reason is that the costs and risks of expanding NATO may be more potential than actual. It is almost as difficult to conjure up Russian security threats to its former Warsaw Pact allies as to the

---

[4]See, for example, Ronald D. Asmus, Richard L. Kugler, and F. Stephen Larrabee, "Building a New NATO," *Foreign Affairs*, September/October 1993, and, also by Asmus, Kugler, and Larrabee, "NATO Expansion: The Next Steps," *Survival*, Spring 1995.

[5]For example, Arnold L. Horelick, *U.S. Interests in Europe and NATO Enlargement*, Statement to the European Subcommittee of the U.S. Senate Foreign Relations Committee, April 17, 1995, Santa Monica, Calif.: RAND, CT-131, 1995.

current members of NATO. (It is easier to visualize Russian threats to the three Baltic states and Ukraine, which were once part of the Soviet Union, which is one reason why they are not serious candidates for NATO membership.) With a minor exception in the isolated Russian enclave of Kaliningrad, nested between Poland and Lithuania, the Visegrad countries, which are the first candidates for NATO, are separated from Russia geographically. As has been noted, the Russian armed forces are in very poor shape, and the Russian economy in no condition to rebuild them.

Thus the guarantees that NATO provides to its members under Articles IV and V of the North Atlantic Treaty can be extended to the states of Central Europe with very little danger in the short run that the Alliance will have to back them up. If the time were to come when the guarantees were called upon, the hard fact is that only then would the guarantors be forced to decide whether to make them good—as indeed was the case even during the Cold War. During the Cold War, the guarantor could, of course, never admit to such an ultimate indeterminacy, although some beneficiaries of the guarantee, notably General de Gaulle, assumed it, publicly and privately. A similar not-quite-certain guarantor-beneficiary relationship will apply to a NATO extended to the east.

The new relationship will necessarily be weaker than the old, however. The real guarantor of the old NATO was the fact that the member nations, including the United States, had an indisputable vital interest in the security of Western Europe. The current western interest in Central European security is and is likely to remain more arguable. Nonetheless, admission of Central European states into NATO will in itself increase the western security interest there, and thus the possibility of intervention in the unlikely case that it is called for.

In the long run, in any case, as the Central European countries become realistically eligible for membership in EU, their security will presumably be based more solidly on some combination of that organization and NATO, but that "long run" is long enough that the new combination need not be designed yet. For now, NATO guarantees to new Central European members should thus be relatively easy, because any need for implementation would in fact be very low probability, and any act of implementation would be contingent upon decisions to be made at the time.

NATO is not merely a set of guarantees, however; it is an ongoing functioning organization. For some aspects of the organization, entry of new members from central Europe should present few problems. NATO functions as military planner—but the introduction of Polish and Czech colonels into military headquarters at Mons should cause no difficulties. It functions as military trainer—but by the summer of 1995, central European troops were already joining American troops in maneuvers in Louisiana. Some aspects of integration, e.g., of central European command structures into NATO, will cause some problems, but these are not likely to be difficult ones.

But NATO also functions as a flesh-and-bones military structure backing up its capabilities with real troops at real bases, and therein could lie the rub. Fundamental to Cold-War NATO was that American, British, Canadian, and even French troops were positioned through West Germany, in the front lines and in reserve, to defend against any Warsaw Pact attack from East Germany and Czechoslovakia. Much thinned out, some are still there, and the intention is that they remain. During the Cold War, they had extensive plans for defense; presumably some sorts of plans for some sorts of contingencies still exist.

The operationally difficult question for a NATO enlarged to include the central European states is whether troops must be moved east from these old bases to the territory of the new members. The dilemma lies in the potential conflict between the answers to two questions:

- Without the extension of NATO bases and NATO troops to the new "front lines" in Poland, the Czech Republic, Slovakia, Hungary, and perhaps even Romania and Bulgaria, would the guarantees be considered serious?

- Would any current member of NATO be willing to incur the costs and even the small trip-wire risks of basing troops in these countries?

The answer to the second question is almost certainly negative. In the United States at least, NATO expansion as a political issue might be kept latent if it involved guarantees alone, but it would certainly be activated by the suggestion of significant costs and dangers. Both President Clinton and most of the Republican candidates for the presidency are committed to expansion, but both parties have isolationist wings. Proposals to put bases in central Europe would make the issue real and almost surely bring about the defeat of expansion.

That leaves the first question: Are bases necessary? The purpose of NATO memberships for central Europe is not to provide real security—objectively, little military insecurity exists. It is to counter the fearful subjective perceptions of the former vassals of the Soviet Union and to help stabilize them by tying them to the West. And it is to do so quickly and cheaply because EU cannot.

The question then is whether guarantees without forces and bases will be viewed as sufficient to deter aggression from the east.[6] Historically, the guarantees extended to Norway since the beginning of the Alliance, and to eastern Germany after reunification, have never been in doubt in spite of the lack of foreign bases or stationed troops in these locales, but the position of new Central European members will inevitably be less solid. What it will come to, as is always the case with deterrence, is a matter of perceptions. It seems possible that NATO guarantees without bases or troops can split the difference sufficiently—that the guarantees will be perceived by Americans as contingent enough to pass muster in the Congress and at the same time be seen by Central Europeans as strong enough to deter any aggressive threat, particularly given the unlikelihood of such a threat. That this will suffice to satisfy the understandably nervous new members in central Europe cannot be certain, but it will be better than nothing.

In any case, the irony of quick NATO membership as a substitute or precursor to slow EU membership for the states of central Europe is that *NATO expansion to the east will be quick and easy to the extent that it is unreal and unnecessary; to the extent that it might incur real costs and risks, it is likely to slow down to the EU pace.*

---

[6]For a detailed political and military discussion, see Asmus, Kugler, and Larrabee (1995), pp. 15–20.

The canonical prediction here is that at least the Visegrad states will be brought into NATO—a NATO of guarantees but no bases—perhaps by 2000. That will provide some of the ties to the West that these states so badly want. What is not likely to happen, however—not at a pace faster than that of entry into EU—is their entry into NATO in a bases-troops-and-trumpets manner that will incur costs as unacceptable as those of a premature expansion of EU.

POSSIBLE NEW MILITARY MISSIONS

The new function adopted by NATO, "Keeping the Central Europeans stable," is not a military mission in the terminology used here. That is not to denigrate it. It is important, but it is at least as politically subtle and as difficult to explain as a rationale for spending substantial amounts of money for military forces as is "Keeping the Americans in." In the stronger versions involving troops and bases as well as guarantees, this would require a new military posture, but the military rationale for such a posture, which would necessarily involve the difficult-to-envisage attack from Russia, seems even more difficult to make believable than the rationale for retaining NATO from where they are now.

NATO's Bosnian Implementation Force (IFOR) may provide a prototype military mission, but if after a year it proves ineffective in Yugoslavia and divisive in the Alliance, it may not be a positive one. Other possibilities exist. The Middle East seems to provide a bottomless source of potential military crises. Some, having to do with oil and the basic balance of power, may well engage NATO. Others, however, concerning Israel and its neighbors, are likely to be of interest mainly to the United States and thus difficult to bring into an Alliance context.

Additionally, to say that Russia no longer presents a military threat to its west is not to imply a zero probability for instability stemming from that still-large agglomeration. Particularly if the Central European states are brought into NATO, but even if they are not, Central European contingencies should be able to engage the planning staffs at Mons. Attention might also be paid to military developments in East Asia. China in particular has the potential eventually to become a military threat anywhere in the world. Whether continuing rapid economic growth will lead it toward or away from posing such a threat is an open question, and it will most likely be decades before such a threat might extend to Western Europe. Even so, military planners have long dealt with contingencies that are less likely and less imminent.

As a set of new missions for NATO, however, such major extensions of NATO's missions would be politically highly controversial while remaining pretty weak tea militarily. Combining the probabilities of specific military contingencies that might threaten vital interests seriously enough to engage NATO's major members is like the mathematical multiplication of "epsilons," minute differences whose product still comes to epsilon. Much more exciting is Samuel Huntington's "Clash of Civilizations,"[7] the coming fundamental conflict between Roman Catholic and Protestant Christianity on one side, and Eastern Orthodox Christianity and Islam on the other. This could provide not merely a new and overwhelming military mission, but a crusade, very nearly in the original usage of the term and indeed not merely for NATO but for Christendom.

If one believes it. In the meantime, however, a combination of even a low level of improbable contingencies multiplying out to a military danger at least worth hedging against, together with the general uncertainty of the future, may have to do as a military rationale. This, plus an increased degree of sophistication in the United States and the rest of the West about vital interests in the mostly political missions of "Keeping the Americans in" and "Keeping the Central Europeans stable," may well serve to maintain NATO for many years to come. Inertia remains strong in any case.

The premise that NATO will remain about as is, is central to the canonical prediction.

---

[7]Samuel P. Huntington, "The Clash of Civilizations," *Foreign Affairs*, Summer 1993.

Chapter Five

THE CANONICAL PREDICTION AND ALTERNATIVES

This chapter summarizes the canonical prediction and then takes up possible economic and security-based variations, favorable and unfavorable. Each of the specified variations seems in itself to be unlikely. Nonetheless, some of them will occur, but because of their individual improbability, it is difficult even to guess at which. Indeed, if the next decade is anything like the past ones, some variations outside this list, including some that most observers now consider "impossible," may well occur.

THE CANON

To summarize the disturbance-free canonical prediction that has stemmed from the discussion so far:

- The economies of the major West European states will grow normally—not slowly enough to cause major social unrest, but not fast enough to make significant inroads on unemployment and related problems. Economic problems will continue to dominate internal politics.

- The governments of these states may change, but the changes will not make for radical shifts in their European or other external policies.

- Although it has been out of the scope of this discussion, the same is most likely true for the United States.

- Economic, security, or other political disturbances stemming from outside the EU/NATO area will not be great enough to cause major changes inside the area. This does not imply the disappearance of threats from the Middle East or elsewhere, just that they will be handled without requiring or engendering restructuring within Western Europe.

- EU will continue to integrate economically, but EMU and the single currency will slip—almost certainly in time, perhaps also in concept.

- Integration of EU security and other political institutions will lag the creation of economic institutions. Substantial change in political structures will only be beginning in the first decade of the new millennium.

- Some but not all of the Visegrad countries will have grown rapidly enough economically to be seen as converging with the members of EU. By 2000, these states will be on clear paths to joining the Union, although it will still take a number of years for them to achieve full membership.

- NATO will have neither expanded its functions nor contracted its military capabilities significantly. It will, however, have increased its membership by 2000 or be on the verge of doing so. A majority of the four most likely states—the Czech Republic, Hungary, Poland, and Slovenia—will become members without basing foreign troops; Bulgaria and Romania will remain outside for a longer time.

The member states of both organizations, EU and NATO, should find such a set of outcomes satisfactory to their vital interests in reasonably prosperous economic growth and stability. For two sets of reasons, however, they are not likely to feel completely comfortable. First, for the United States and for the Europeans, perhaps more for the former, the morality of not doing much if anything about successor disturbances to Bosnia and Rwanda will continue to be disturbing. Even though Western stability would be easy enough to insulate against outside chaos, a disturbed conscience can have real political consequences. And second, even though the world will remain relatively stable through 2000–2005 (by the canonical assumption), fears of future threats—from Islam, from China, from wherever—will loom ever larger throughout the period.

Nonetheless, any attempt to do better, economically or politically, will run the risk of failure and consequently doing worse, perhaps a lot worse. The next sections take up economic variations from the canonical prediction, then security-based variations. The discussion under each of those two headings deals first with potential optimistic variations and then with those on the downside.

ECONOMIC VARIATIONS FROM THE CANON

Doing Better Economically

One way to do better economically would be for the United States, and EU or its individual members, to undertake **deliberately stimulative macroeconomic policies—fiscal and monetary steps designed to accelerate growth and reduce unemployment and inequality.** This has been advocated elsewhere by the author of this analysis,[1] and to avoid turning the discussion here into a short tract on something that has been done at greater length and more carefully, it is treated agnostically here.

In fact, for political reasons and perhaps good economic ones, the probability of moving in this policy direction is very low. Some of the economic issues are technical: Can expansionary macroeconomic policies increase growth and cut unemployment, or will the effects be quickly dissipated in accelerated inflation? Other issues depend in large measure on political value judgments: What is the appropriate balance of gains and risks between decreasing unemployment and increasing inflation?

Additionally, for any single state acting alone, such a stimulative policy would require some degree of economic insulation from competitors. That is not impossible even for a member of EU, as has been demonstrated by the British and Italian departures from EMS, but it would be politically very difficult for France and other states that place great weight on continued EU integration. Meanwhile,

---

[1]See Robert A. Levine, *Economic Stimulus: A Political Economist's Manifesto*, Santa Monica, Calif.: RAND, P-7838, 1993, which makes the case for fiscal stimulus largely in terms of the United States. Robert A. Levine, "Keynesianism May Be Just What Wealthy Industrial Nations Need," *Los Angeles Times*, June 15, 1995 p. D2, expands the argument to Europe and Japan.

integration itself will continue to impose constraints rather than providing stimulus. Even though the Bundesbank finally lowered German interest rates to defend against economic downturn in 1995 and 1996, it is unlikely to go so far as to encourage accelerated growth actively in the face of even slight inflation danger. As for the United States, serious stimulative macroeconomic policy will remain politically impossible, lacking substantial erosion of the strong national consensus that budget balancing must take priority over all else.

Thus, no reversals toward stimulative national policies are on the horizon. Collective international stimulation, which would be preferable, is even less probable.

Perhaps a more likely variation is **a spontaneous acceleration of growth and improvement in the economies of the United States and EU.** As policy economists must frequently relearn, governments do not control everything. Private economic entrepreneurship, taking advantage of national or international opportunities, could set off a boom. Unfortunately, however, this also must be deemed unlikely, for two reasons. The first may be simply a failure of economic vision—nothing can be seen on the horizon, so nothing seems likely to occur; given the record of economic forecasting, that may still leave some hope. Second, however, even a spontaneous boom might well be cut off at the ankles because of the inflationary fears of the Federal Reserve and the Bundesbank. Nonetheless, this variation cannot be dismissed.

Another possibility is that **structural changes in European economies will be effective in reducing unemployment.** Structural changes are needed and are taking place, albeit not very fast or very thoroughly. The problem for France and other countries, however, is that even the best-designed and best-implemented changes of this type would take time to work their way—time that is likely to be longer, for example, than that left before the next elections.

Equally improbable is **maintenance of the officially projected pace toward European monetary and other economic integration in spite of national concerns,** thus achieving a single currency and a full EMU in this millennium, as initially intended by Maastricht. Germany, France, and many of the smaller members of EU still favor it in principle. The installation of a Labour government, or even better a Labour-Liberal Democrat coalition, in the UK could reduce the opposition there, but for reasons discussed, the likelihood remains low.

All in all, the possibility of upside economic variations seems rather thin, and the canonical version is in itself rather optimistic. This is reinforced by consideration of the downside.

Doing Worse Economically

One easy way to fall back from the stable progress of the canon would be for the **economic progress to be so slow as to engender political instability.** One example of this, discussed above, is the possibility of a failure by France's Chirac-Juppé government to re-duce unemployment significantly below 10 percent.   It was suggested that continued high unemployment could lead to victory of a center-left majority in the 1998 legislative elections, which would mean a period of uncomfortable *cohabitation* between President Chirac on the right and a new prime minister and government on the left; to establishment of Le Pen's far right *Front National* as a balance-of-power party with substantial bargaining power; and/or to a new outbreak of the recurring French political disturbances last manifest in 1968 and perhaps presaged again by the events of December 1995.   Each of these outcomes has the potential for making things even worse within France by increasing immobilism and polarization. Each of them has the potential for slowing down European economic and political integration; some of them might even initiate a breakup of current integration. Neither is this true only for France. Germany seems more stable currently, with even *Ossi-Wessi* tensions waning; as in Britain, a change of government would   probably   have   little   European   or   international   effect. Nonetheless, problems with immigration and assimilation, and the interplay of these with neo-Nazism, could shake this benign stability, as could failure of eastern reconstruction to maintain a steady upward trend or a growing weariness of *Wessis* with paying the bills into an indefinite future.

All of these problems would become far worse if, rather than slow progress, **European economies were hit by a significant economic downturn. Such a downturn in the remaining years of the 1990s is**

the single greatest threat to West European stability, integration, and perhaps even peace. True, Europe has had its cyclical downturns in the half-century since the end of World War II, but after self-help and the Marshall Plan reestablished basic structures, each downturn followed a period of substantial prosperity. This time, European economies are relatively high on the business cycle, but by some measures, particularly unemployment, they are not prosperous. In 1996, they began to turn down again; in spite of rote official predictions of a short shallow dip, how long and how deep it will be is by no means clear.

Historical analogies are dangerous, but in many ways Europe in 1928 may provide an appropriate metaphor. Because the United States had a young and vigorously growing economy in the 1920s, most Americans do not recognize that it was not a good decade for Europe. Continental economies were soured by the repercussions of World War I reparations and loans; hyperinflation in Germany was followed by underemployment. In Britain, unemployment stayed above 10 percent for the decade *before* the Great Depression, in large measure because of the unwise orthodoxy of Chancellor of the Exchequer Churchill and his experts, who insisted on returning to the gold standard too soon and at too high a value for sterling.[2] Such orthodoxy is matched now by the tight money doctrines of the Bundesbank, by *le franc fort*, by the budget-balancing hysteria of the U.S. Congress and administration, and by the inability or unwillingness of Japan to reverse its national recession.

If European unemployment rates were to head not toward 10 but toward 15 percent—because of the natural forces of the business cycle, the failures of European policy, or tsunamis from Japan or a United States driven into recession by an unwillingness to increase deficits— all bets on stability and integration would be off. The one saving grace is that, even if the 2000s were to resemble the 1930s, the 2010s would be unlikely to look like the 1940s. World War III will not begin across the Rhine or even the Bug. Perhaps because of the threat of nuclear escalation it will not take place at all; warfare has changed more than economics during the 20th century.

---

[2] See John Maynard Keynes' essay, *The Economic Consequences of Mr. Churchill*, 1925.

The third economic failure mode is **the failure of monetary union to jell, so that EU remained about where it was in the mid-1990s with little prospect of further integration in the near term and with a significant chance of moving into reverse.** This might come about either by a move back toward nationalism within a major member state or as the result of a stubbornness about compromise, particularly by German defenders of the deutsche mark. It might also happen as the result of the dynamics of the slowdown that has already begun. A freeze of integration would not be uniformly seen as a "failure," at least if it did not lead to reversal. Britain's current Conservative government would count it as a marked success, and a future government of either party might well feel quite comfortable with such an outcome. So would many individuals within countries favoring integration.[3] The United States would, and should, be neutral about such an outcome arrived at by the members of EU. It would, nonetheless, run against the official objectives of the Union itself and most of its member states, so it is listed here on the downside.

The **failure of some or all Central European economies to grow at a relatively rapid and smooth pace could have two sorts of negative consequences for Western Europe.** First, the failure of convergence with EU, would mean either an EU decision to change the criteria to admit Central European nations anyhow or their seemingly permanent relegation to second-class status within Europe. The former seems very unlikely, although if Western Europe were to regain a great deal of economic buoyancy and optimism, it might be possible to admit them as Spain, Portugal, and Greece were admitted. Outsider status might be very destabilizing, although some ground might be regained by admission into NATO. Second, poverty in central Europe, added to likely continued poverty in Russia and certain continued poverty in many other parts of the world, particularly when televised, will put pressures on Western Europe (and the United States) that will be difficult to ignore.

---

[3]For example, Allais, the French economist.

SECURITY-BASED VARIATIONS FROM THE CANON

Two qualifications should be noted at the outset of this listing. First, the security situation postulated by the canonical prediction is quite favorable: Western Europe is stable internally and unthreatened in any fundamental way from the outside. Thus, the upside variations listed may not appear significantly better than the canon. Second, consistent with the overall thesis here, security considerations are likely to take second place to economic ones, so that, except for the worst downside possibilities, they may have less effect on overall structures.

Doing Better on Security

Internal stabilization of Russia, accompanied by agreement to partnership with a NATO expanded to include former Warsaw Pact members. The stability is more important to the West than the partnership. Together, the two could damp down even further the fears, already at low levels, of some sort of nuclear instability or political mischief stemming from Russia.

Settling down of the Balkans. This would require an end to the Yugoslav wars without their having lapped over into neighboring states such as Albania, Hungary, or Greece, as has been feared. Together with final stabilization of other potential disputes, e.g., between Hungary and Romania over treatment of Hungarian minorities, this would remove another source of potential instability. If the former Yugoslavia can be not only pacified but stabilized—a large "if"—the civil wars of the 1990s may become not a precursor, but a caveat for other Balkan nationalists.

Reduction of instability and threats in the Middle East and Maghreb. This would be more difficult, if more important to world stability. To be relatively complete, it would have to include settlement of the Israeli-Palestinian conflict in a way satisfactory not only to both sides but to Syria and ultimately to other currently strongly anti-Israel Moslem states; replacement of Saddam Hussein by a successor who is easier to deal with; subordination of Iranian revolutionary activities and ideologies to externally aided internal economic improvement; no destabilization of areas now considered relatively stable, such as Egypt, Saudi Arabia, Morocco, and Turkey;

and confining of "Islamic fundamentalism," wherever it appears or even triumphs, to internal reconstruction without external aggression. This is a long and difficult list.

Successfully attempted reconstruction of NATO. The canonical prediction is in some ways unsatisfactory on the security side, as well as that of economics and unemployment:

- It leaves NATO without a strong military rationale.

- It lacks a politically satisfactory "vision."

- It includes no explicit promises to combat either extreme instability or intolerable moral horror in areas of concern to Western Europe and the United States.

- It is ad hoc rather than being planned.

- It runs the risk of falling backward because it is not moving forward.

One summation of the case for dissatisfaction with the resulting political "stasis" of the Alliance contends "that if the transatlantic bargain is to last, it will need a grander objective than the prudent management of turbulent exogenous factors. The presentation of this policy, at least, will have to be more exalted, even if its reality boils down to that."[4]

To provide such a "grand objective" and thus avoid crumbling through sheer boredom, various proposals have been made, still largely informally, to reconstruct NATO with an explicit worldwide mission, centering on Europe but not confined there. Returning to a metaphor used in the discussion of economic variations, the object would be to avoid the 1930s and the 1940s—in this case, not the economic disaster but the appeasement and failure of collective security that led to World War II. Without evaluating this new worldwide mission here, were the Alliance to take it on and take it seriously enough to meet the first inevitable challenges in Europe or elsewhere, that would help revivify NATO and pull it away from the potential crumbling that could stem from existence without a vision.

---

[4]Olivier Debouzy, private letter commenting on an earlier draft of this report.

The difficulty, however, is that, under current conditions, "outside questions" are likely to be solved "only for internal reasons" in de Tocqueville's terms, so that such a pulling together of the Alliance around a new mission would be extremely difficult. The downside of having tried and failed is discussed in the next section on "Doing Worse."

Doing Worse on Security

The inability to meet a substantial threat, on or outside NATO borders, will lead to a belief in the irrelevance of the Alliance and to consequent crumbling. In the mid-1990s, alarm was raised over the possibility that NATO, having failed to end the Yugoslav wars, would be forced to deal with their spillover into Albania, Hungary, or Greece and would fail equally there. In spite of the drawing back together of the Alliance in 1995 and 1996, the possibility of a new falling out remains, particularly if the Bosnian action fails to restore some degree of stability. The pre-summer-of-1995 problem in Yugoslavia was not a shortfall of NATO military capacity but doubts about the political capability to intervene successfully in anything as complicated as the Yugoslav civil wars and a lack of consensus about what to do or whom to do it to, or whether outsiders had the right or duty to do anything at all. Questions like these led to tensions in the Alliance. On the time horizon here, a challenge that could overwhelm NATO military capabilities should go into the "impossible" category (which does not mean either that it will not happen or that a militarily containable challenge might not overwhelm NATO's political will). Eventually, China or a resurrected Russian "evil empire" might pose such a threat, but not by or near 2005. However, more immediate political problems that are difficult to cope with may abound, and Alliance unity may be tested by some such, e.g., conflicts between Israel and its neighbors or situations in the Far East where the United States feels involved but its allies do not. Continual tests of this sort did little harm during the Cold War, but lacking the strong common enemy of that era, they could now lead to significant weakening of the fabric.

Fear of such weakening has been a major motivation for the desire to reconstruct NATO—to plan in advance to deal with the difficulties around the world on an Alliance basis, so that they will not bring about crises when they occur. But **unsuccessfully attempted reconstruction of NATO** can leave the Alliance worse off than not having tried. It will be very difficult to enlarge NATO's mission in the abstract, on the basis of logic about future contingencies. Current contingencies that some member states wish the organization had never taken on are causing enough problems for governments that would rather turn inward to solve their own problems. Under these circumstances, the reconstruction attempt itself may cause a crisis.

During the Cold War, the French were fond of such Cartesian crises, induced by their felt need to solve abstract problems, in particular to reassert their Gaullist nationalism. In the late 1980s, for example, as arms control agreement verged on becoming real for the first time, much bitterness was engendered by French objections to being represented by NATO in military matters, since France belonged to that organization politically but not militarily. The French felt safe in raising such an issue because of their anchor to windward—the mutual knowledge on the part of France and its allies that France was as devoted to the overwhelmingly important defensive objective of NATO as anyone else.

The threat from the East no longer exists, and an attempt to enlarge NATO's mission, if taken seriously and pressed hard by the United States or any other member nation, would be likely to fail, with the failure itself bringing about an unnecessary Alliance crisis at a time it was not needed.

A specific danger that might stem from an unnecessary abstract crisis over "strengthening" NATO by enlarging its mission would be **a revival of American anti-European isolationism, either in one of its two historical forms, worldwide or Pacific-first, or as a newer-style unilateralism.** The Alliance crisis over what to do in Bosnia pushed some Americans in that direction. Paradoxically, the desire in the United States to do something for the victimized Bosnians might seem anything but isolationist, but it tended to turn that way. A large majority of members of both parties in both houses of the Congress favored a proposal, not to send U.S. troops to help Bosnia, but to lift the embargo on sending arms to that embattled government so that *someone* could arm them without explicitly involving the United States. This was to be done regardless of the cost to our closest NATO allies, a strong and bitter recipe for Alliance weakening, which fortunately became obsolete before it became real. It became mostly moot with NATO's 1995 intervention, but remained at least in residual form in the issue of training and arming Bosnian government forces during the scheduled year of U.S. presence.

Even more salient to U.S. politics, Americans really do want to concern themselves with their national (or increasingly, their personal) problems and have little stomach for international adventures, even of the most benign and humanitarian type. *U.S. isolationism may be the single greatest threat to NATO, to transatlantic collective security, and to maintenance of the vital interests of both the United States and Western Europe in continuing the American role as an active participant in the area.*

SUMMARY: THE RANGE OF POSSIBILITIES

Table 1 summarizes the canonical prediction and the pessimistic and optimistic variations that have been discussed.

Any reading of the table, particularly an attempt to balance the downside risks against the upside opportunities, must be quite subjective and heuristic.

Nonetheless, what both the table and the analysis it summarizes appear to show is that the risks dominate the opportunities, in terms both of probabilities and of consequences if they do come to pass. Some of the economic risks in particular—a sharp downturn and/or a failure of central European economic growth—are far from impossible and likely to create dire instabilities and other very negative results were they to occur. The opportunities on the other hand, or at least those that appear politically feasible, are primarily for marginal improvements.

In other words, the canon may not be the best of all possible worlds, but it may be the best of all probable ones.

Table 1

The Canon and Its Variations

Downside Variations	Canonical Prediction	Upside Variations
Growth so slow as to cause political instability	Slow, stable economic growth	
Sharp economic downturn, engendering domestic and foreign policy instability		Policy-induced or spontaneous, macro- or microeconomically based, rapid growth
	Stable foreign policies	
Out-of-area problems out of hand	Coping with out-of-area problems	Reduction of out-of-area instability
Failure of Monetary Union	Slow economic, followed by political, integration of EU	Accelerated monetary and economic integration
Failure of Central European states to grow fast enough	Membership of some Visegrad states in NATO; initial convergence with EU	
Crumbling of NATO	NATO structure and military capabilities remaining constant	Revivification of NATO by successful adoption of worldwide mission
Failed reconstruction of NATO		
Renewed U.S. isolationism		

Chapter Six

POLICY IMPLICATIONS

The central implication of this analysis is that

- Western Europe and the Atlantic relationship are both stable and most likely to remain that way. The two central criteria for policy, therefore, should be

  — Do no harm. Do not destabilize.

  — Hedge against prospective instabilities.

Some specific implications for both the United States and Western Europe are

- Be alert for any signs of serious economic downturn and be prepared to act against them, quickly and internationally.

- Extend as much help as possible, in terms of both trade and aid, to Central European economic growth and convergence with EU. To some extent, this applies to Russia too, but the problems are greater, the possibilities are more limited, and EU membership apparently precluded at least for a very long time.

- Cherish NATO as it is, as a stable vehicle for keeping the United States engaged in Europe, and be wary of damaging it by trying to improve it.

- Be alert for any signs of specific serious security threats from out of area and be prepared to act against them, quickly and internationally.

For the United States,

- Western Europe remains a central—perhaps still the single most important—vital interest. Be careful of damaging the relationship in the name of transitory political or even moral objectives, particularly those expressed primarily by slogans.

For Western Europe,

- Cherish EU as a vigorous ongoing organization, growing at a natural pace toward economic and political integration, but
  - Do not push political integration faster than the economics will support.
  - Search for ways to encourage growth, as well as price stability, within the Union.
  - See the development of EU as complementary with, not an alternative to, the maintenance of a North Atlantic community of interest.
- If American leadership is needed, be prepared to follow.

The future is neither grim nor inspiring, but it is potentially dangerous. It is to avoiding these dangers that policy must first be addressed.